Candyce Copp Grisham

DRESDEN QUILT BLOCKS
Reimagined

Sew Your Own Playful Plates

25 Elements to Mix & Match

C&T PUBLISHING

Publisher: Amy Marson
Creative Director: Gailen Runge
Acquisitions Editor: Roxane Cerda
Managing Editor: Liz Aneloski
Editor: Beth Baumgartel
Technical Editor/Illustrator: Linda Johnson
Cover/Book Designer: April Mostek
Production Coordinator: Zinnia Heinzmann
Production Editor: Alice Mace Nakanishi
Photo Assistant: Rachel Holmes
Photography by Kelly Burgoyne of C&T Publishing, Inc., unless otherwise noted

Published by C&T Publishing, Inc., P.O. Box 1456, Lafayette, CA 94549

Library of Congress Cataloging-in-Publication Data
Names: Grisham, Candyce Copp, 1954- author.
Title: Dresden quilt blocks reimagined : sew your own playful plates : 25 elements to mix & match / Candyce Copp Grisham.
Description: Lafayette, CA : C&T Publishing, Inc., [2019]
Identifiers: LCCN 2018054532 | ISBN 9781617457937 (soft cover)
Subjects: LCSH: Dresden plate quilts. | Quilting--Patterns. | Patchwork quilts.
Classification: LCC TT835 .G764 2019 | DDC 746.46/041--dc23
LC record available at https://lccn.loc.gov/2018054532

Printed in China
10 9 8 7 6 5 4

Dedication

I dedicate this book to my wonderful husband, Tom, for his unending support. He put up with the dining room being turned into an office and with hours of sewing and editing. He has always had my back.

Acknowledgments

Thank you to my mom for giving me her Singer sewing machine (oh so many years ago) and sending me to sewing classes.

Thank you to all the generations of women in my family who have sewn and inspired me.

Thank you to Jane and Jennie who encouraged me to go to Quilt Market and talk to the publishers and editors.

Thank you to all my students who have loved the classes and continue to astound me with their results.

Thank you to my dear quilting friends who helped me sew blocks, quilts, and bindings.

Thank you to the editorial staff at C&T Publishing for their belief in me, their guidance, and their professionalism—with a special thank-you to Beth for making me look good, understanding my notes and writing, and answering all my questions.

Contents

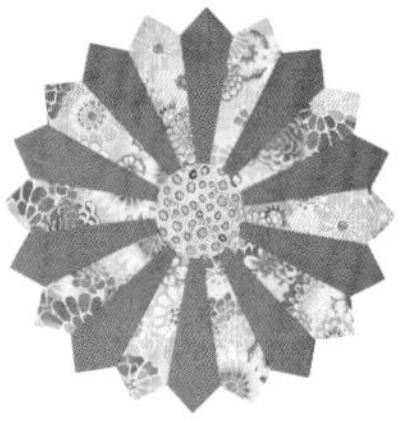

EXPANDING AND EXPLORING *the dresden plate quilt block*

Why This Book? Why This Block?

I love everything that is old that can be made new again, and that certainly applies to the Dresden quilt block. This is my first Dresden plate quilt and the beginning of my exploration of this beautiful and versatile quilt block.

You can use all and any of the 25 design elements featured in this book, including the four different edge treatments, the range of size possibilities (2″ to 9″), and the amazing variations of traditional and nontraditional quilting patterns, from the Sawtooth to the Flying Geese. Mix it up even more by fabric piecing wedges and introducing up to twenty different colors and patterns for each of the wedges needed to make a single block. And don't forget to think about using color and pattern to make the center! Enjoy the options and the freedom to design with color, pattern, and shape.

My original goal was to create Dresden blocks by machine with as many different edge treatments as possible, including the straight, pointed, curved and three-sided variations. What happened was an explosion of blocks in different edges, fabrics, and designs—a modern translation of a traditional block. Layouts made the design appear both unique and contemporary. The color combinations were endless, and each new plate was a thrill. I started mixing the edges, making pieced strips to cut apart, adding fun centers, layering the plates, and overlapping the edges. Eventually, I appliquéd my first Dresden block to a pieced background and the result became the basis for my Dresden explorations and teaching. This book is designed to guide the maker through his or her own endless possible renditions of the Dresden block.

Dresden blocks were named after the Dresden porcelain made during the romantic Victorian period in the late 1800s. Dresden quilt plates from the 1920s and 1930s were made with floral prints and the curved edges finished by needle-turn appliqué. They were then set onto blocks and pieced in traditional settings. My goal was to expand and blow up this idea so anyone could make a Dresden block for traditional or contemporary settings.

My Flower Plates, 38″ × 54″, by Candyce Copp Grisham

The basic structure of the circular Dresden plate comes from cutting and piecing twenty wedges. In addition to complete and detailed instructions for making a basic Dresden block, this book also covers advanced block piecing, design layouts, backgrounds, and troubleshooting. It features a gallery of completed inspirational projects.

Any confident beginner can make the Dresden blocks. It takes only few guidelines for mastering the basic block; once you learn them, follow your heart. I bet you can't make just one!

Have fun!

Candy

THE BASICS OF THE *dresden wedge and plate*

Before you get started, the best way to use this book is to read through this chapter first. It includes an introduction to the supplies you'll need, a section on how to select fabrics, and even a section on how to cut the wedges. The following chapters take you through the construction and creative processes of sewing different edge finishes, creating edge combinations, varying the size of the blocks, and finishing the centers. Beyond that, there's the opportunity to move on to Dresden 201: Pieced Designs (page 34), which delves into extra piecing and even more variations! Ultimately, this book provides guidance for you to make your own final project based on your choices and personal preferences.

Quilting supplies for making Dresden plates:

1. Pressing bar
2. Rotary rotating mat (*optional*)
3. Freezer paper sheets (for center templates)
4. Foundation paper (for Flying Geese Dresdens)
5. Roll of freezer paper
6. Nonstick pressing sheet
7. Creative Grids 18° Dresden ruler with circle
8. Nonwoven lightweight fusible interfacing
9. Nonwoven interfacing (for Dresden centers)
10. Alex Anderson's 4-in-1 Essential Sewing Tool
11. 60 mm or 45 mm rotary cutter (for straight cutting)
12. 28 mm rotary cutter (for curved cutting)
13. Point turner
14. Alignment tool
15. Scissors
16. Circles of lightweight fusible interfacing
17. Clipping tool

Tools and Supplies

For some specific product recommendations, see Resources (page 78).

Beyond your sewing machine, the list of necessary supplies is short. You might own many items already. You need a good steam iron, ironing board, and general sewing supplies, such as neutral-colored thread and straight pins. A ¼″ presser foot and even one with an edge guide can come in handy, as well as a design wall. A *design wall* is a wall or surface that has batting or flannel attached to it and allows you to move fabric elements around to visualize the layout.

The Wedge Ruler

A wedge-shaped ruler is the key to making the perfect Dresden block. You have several good choices. The Creative Grids 18° Dresden Plate Quilt Ruler and the Wrights Easy Dresden Quilting Ruler are very accurate. The Creative Grids ruler also includes a 3½″ circle for making block centers.

The Dresden blocks featured in this book are made from 20 *wedges* that are cut from fabric strips and then sewn together. The wedge shapes are cut at an 18° angle, using an acrylic ruler. To understand the size and number of wedges you need to make these blocks, a little geometry lesson is in order. A complete circle is 360°. Cutting a circle every 18° results in 20 wedges (360° ÷ 18 = 20). This means that 20 wedges are needed to complete a Dresden plate when an 18° ruler is used. If the angle of the ruler is changed to 15°, for example, the Dresden would require 24 wedges (360° ÷ 15 = 24); for a 9° ruler, 40 wedges are needed (360° ÷ 9 = 40).

For the purpose of our exploration into Dresden plates, we will use the 18° ruler exclusively.

The next most important measurement to consider is the wedge size. The size of the wedge is defined as its height or length, and it determines the overall size of final plate. The measurements marked vertically up the face of the Dresden ruler correspond to the various wedge sizes. Once the wedge size has been determined, fabric strips are cut to that size. A strip is cut from width of fabric (WOF). From a fat quarter (FQ), the strip will be 22″ long; from yardage, 40″ long. Multiple wedges can be cut from fabric strips. The length of the strip determines the number of wedges that can be cut.

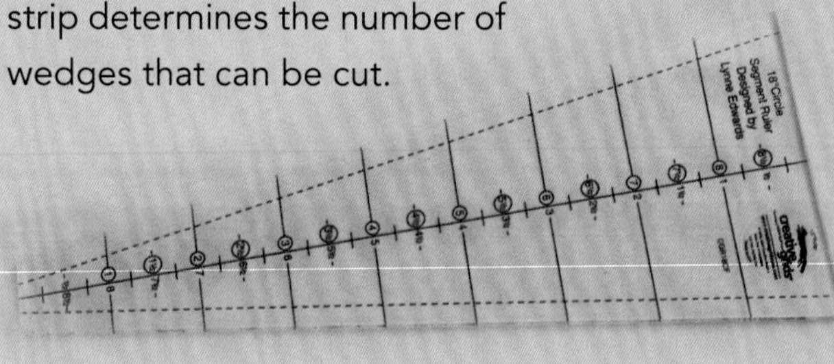

This 18° wedge ruler shows measurements from 1″ to 9″.

Fabric Choices

Begin your Dresden journey with high-quality fabrics that you love. A collection or grouping of coordinating fabrics is a good way to start. Pick fabrics that contrast in color, print size, and value. I believe "more is better," so I have quite a collection of different fabrics. Start your collection with pieces of fabric such as fat quarters, quarter- and half-yards, larger cuts of fabrics, or even fabric scraps. The fabrics are cut into strips the desired size of the wedge (see Cutting Wedges, page 13) or they are pieced to equal the desired size of the wedge (see Dresden 201: Pieced Designs, page 34).

tip It is difficult to determine how much yardage to buy unless you already know the number of blocks you plan to make, how large they will be, and how many times you plan to repeat a fabric. I usually tell students to start with full ¼-yard cuts of six to ten fabrics and go from there.

Kaffe Fassett fabrics

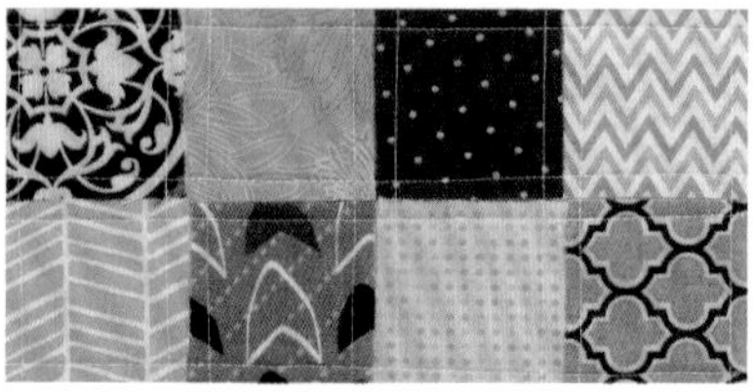

Yellow and gray fabrics

Contemporary fabrics

Keep a few things in mind when choosing fabrics:

- Wait until the Dresden blocks are made to select the background fabrics.
- Contrast in value or print is important when combining fabrics to ensure the fabric designs are visible. However, if a plate that is stitched to the background already has a color or print that is too strong or isn't working, you can always cover it up by layering plates over the top.
- Mix in some fabrics that read solid for contrast.
- Fabrics can be fussy cut for any of the components. The centers of the blocks are an excellent place to fussy cut a special motif or design.

Keep in mind that fabric selection involves *color*, *value*, *print*, and *scale* and that plates can be made from one, two, three, four, five, ten, or twenty different fabrics. A few examples of Dresden plates created with different fabric quantities follow.

- A **single fabric** makes a very uniform plate that's good for a background or a middle layer.

- The choice of **two medium- to high-contrast fabrics** is the basis for many designs. It is a good idea to vary value, print size, and often color. Don't be afraid to mix things up. Use stripes and directional fabrics. If you don't like the result, you can add another plate on top.

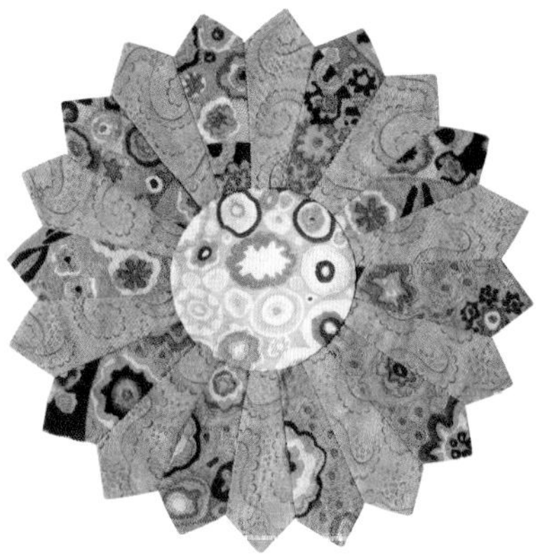

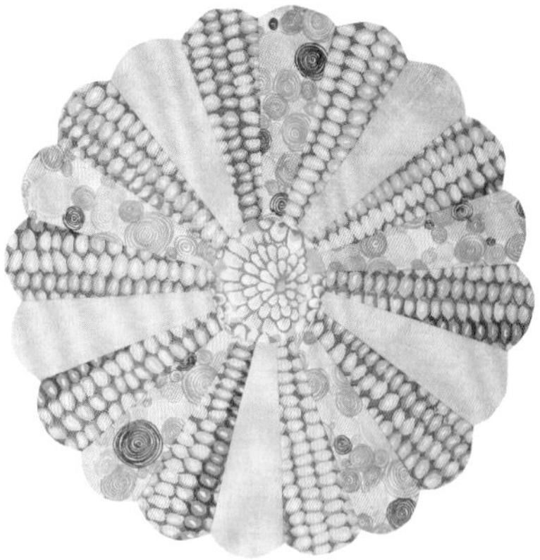

- Deciding to use *three fabrics* may seem like an error, but together they make a very striking combination. Combine ten wedges of Fabric A and five wedges each of Fabrics B and C. Lay out the plate in the following pattern to complete the circle:

  A-B A-C A-B A-C

  It is very important to lay out the wedges before sewing to maintain the desired order as you sew. Contrast here is important.

- Selecting *four fabrics* (five wedges of each) is a lovely way to use a fabric bundle or really have some fun with combinations of print scale and color. Don't be afraid to add solids.

- Opting for *five fabrics* (four wedges each) is a good way to use small bits or scraps of fabric when you don't have enough for an entire plate. Offset four of the fabrics with an eye-catching fifth for a Compass Rose effect (page 45). You can even add a sixth fabric for the center.

- *Ten fabrics* (two wedges each) can be easily gathered from scraps or almost any fabric combination.

- The use of *twenty fabrics* takes some planning and can be a combination of scraps or leftover cuts. This choice is vibrant and dynamic and the basis for a scrappy quilt.

Planning and Cutting Wedges

Planning the design and cutting the wedges might be the most time-consuming part of making any Dresden block, but it is also a lot of fun!

For our purposes, all full-circle plates start with twenty wedges cut with an 18° ruler. Plates made as half- or quarter-circles use ten or five wedges. No matter the number of wedges, accurate rulers and accurate cutting are key to the best results. It is always a good idea to lay out the whole plate before sewing. Do not be concerned if the narrow ends don't line up; they will be covered later by the center. Once the plates are finished, they are "appliquéd" to a background fabric by hand, using an appliqué stitch or by machine using an invisible appliqué or decorative stitch (see Attaching Plates to the Background, page 32).

tip For easy handling, beginning plate makers might want to start by working with two fabrics and wedges cut from 6″ width-of-fabric (WOF) strips.

Cutting Wedges

The following instructions are for 6″ wedges, cut from two different fabrics. These cutting instructions are universal and apply to wedges of all sizes between 3″ and 9″. Smaller wedges can certainly be cut, but they require careful piecing and pressing. Wedges larger than 9″ can be cut using a straight ruler to extend the cutting line of the ruler (see Extending the Size of the Wedge, page 59). A strip is cut from width of fabric (WOF). From a fat quarter, the strip will be 22″ long; from yardage, 40″ long.

1. From each of *two fabrics* cut a 6″-WOF strip from a fat quarter (22″ edge) or from yardage (40″).

2. Layer the two fabric strips with the right sides together (RST).

3. Beginning at the right-hand end of the strips, place the narrow end of the ruler at the lower edge of the fabric. The top edge of the fabric should line up with the 6″ mark on the ruler.

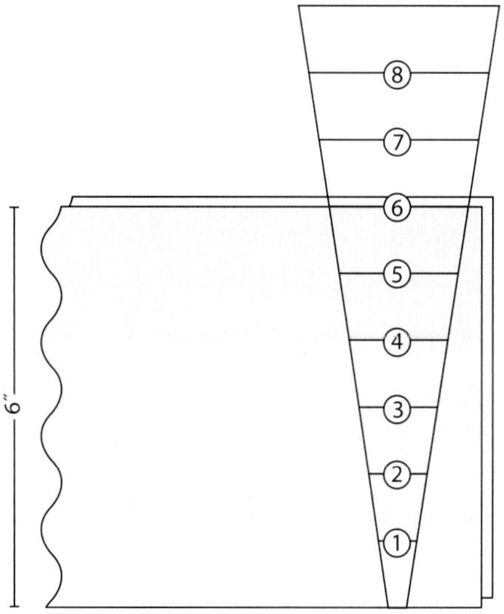

First cut to establish the angled edge.

4. Cut off the right end of the fabrics and discard. Turn the layered strips around 180°.

5. On the strip's left-hand side, line the ruler up with the angled cut, keeping the narrow end of the ruler on what is now the top edge of the fabric strips. Cut along the right-hand side of the ruler.

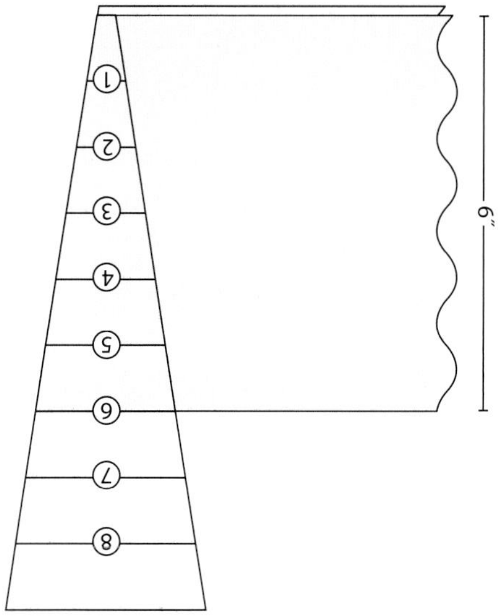

Second cut

6. Rotate the ruler around to line up the left edge of the ruler again to the just-cut angled edge; the narrow end of the ruler now aligns to the bottom edge of the strip. Make another cut on the right-hand side. Continue to flip the ruler 180° to make cuts the length of the fabric for a total of ten pairs of wedges. All full-circle Dresden plates have twenty wedges.

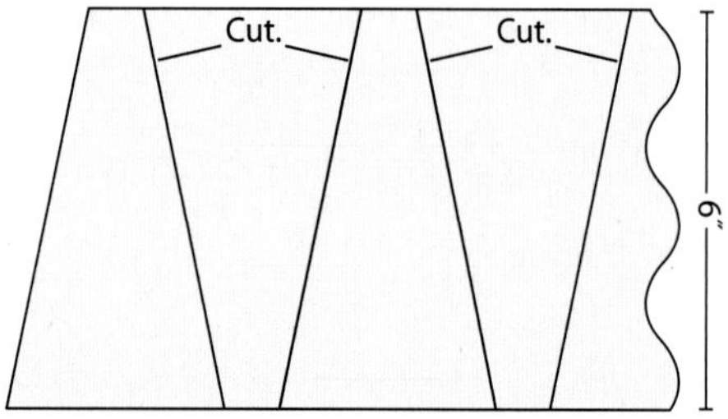

Once you have the wedge pairs cut, refer to the instructions in Dresden Plate Edges and Centers (page 16) for creating the various edges, piecing the wedges into a plate, and finishing the centers of the Dresdens.

PLATE SIZES AND TRADITIONAL BACKGROUNDS

The finished plate size is determined by the size of the wedge. In turn, the finished size of the plate determines the size of a traditional background square.

Wedge size	Plate size	Unfinished background square	Finished block size
2″	6½″	8½″	8″
2½″	7½″	9½″	9″
3″	8½″	10½″	10″
3½″	9½″	11½″	11″
4″	10½″	12½″	12″
4½″	11½″	13½″	13″
5″	12½″	14½″	14″
5½″	13⅓″	15½″	15″
6″	14″	16½″	16″
6½″	14½″	17½″	17″
7″	15″	18½″	18″
7½″	15½″	19½″	19″
8″	16½″	20½″	20″
8½″	18½″	21½″	21″
9″	19½″	22½″	22″
9½″	20″	23½″	23″

WEDGE YIELD PER STRIP

Wedge size and strip size	Wedges per strip	
	FQ strip 22″	WOF strip 40″*
3″	16	32**
4″	13	26**
5″	12	24
6″	10	21
7″	10	20
7½″	9	19
8″	9	19
9″	8	17

** Use ¼ yard (see ** for exceptions).*
*** Use ⅛ yard.*

Let's Do the Math

An example:

You have decided on a 16½″ Dresden using 4 fabrics. Looking at the Plate Sizes and Traditional Backgrounds chart (previous page), a 16½″ Dresden requires 8″ wedges. **How many wedges are needed from each fabric?** To make 20 wedges in 4 fabrics means that each fabric will repeat 5 times in the plate. Therefore, you will need to cut 5 wedges from an 8″-wide strip in 4 different fabrics.

The next question is, **how much of each fabric will you need?** Refer to the Wedge Yield per Strip chart (above) for the answer. The chart reveals that an FQ of each fabric will work since each 8″-wide strip produces 9 wedges, which exceeds the number of wedges you need. In short, a 4-fabric 16½″ plate requires 5 wedges be cut from each of 4 FQs.

If you change the number of fabrics to only 2, your wedge count increases to 10 for each fabric. In this case, you can choose to cut 2 strips 8″ wide from the FQ or use ¼ yard of fabric. Note: At least 2 strips 22″ wide can be cut from a FQ for wedge sizes 7″ to 9″; more for sizes 3″ to 6″.

Whatever combination of plate size and number of fabrics desired, these charts will guide you to the correct wedge size and the amount of fabric necessary to make a 20-wedge plate.

DRESDEN PLATE
edges and centers

There are several ways to shape the outside edge of each wedge to create a variety of finished plates. The edges can be straight for a smooth circle; pointed; pointed, using two wedges at a time to create a larger point; curved; or three-sided. Plates within a single quilt can feature a single edge or a mixture of edges; edges within a single plate can even be mixed.

Edge variations:

1. Twenty-pointed plate

2. Ten-pointed and curved-edge plate

3. Three-sided edge plate

4. Curved-edge plate

5. Serendipity plate

6. Twenty-pointed plate layered on top of Serendipity plate

7. Twenty-pointed edge on a Split-Wedge plate

Edge Variations

All the plates featured in this book require a sewing machine to complete the edges. The variety of different edge treatments and plate sizes allows for many, many variations of Dresden plates.

All seams are ¼″ and pressed open unless otherwise noted.

Straight-Edge Plate

The straight edge makes a beautiful round plate. This plate is good to use as a base layer in one color or as a wonderful way to show off stripes or bold prints. This is the *only* plate for which the wedges are sewn together before the edge is finished.

Construction

1. To cut ten wedge pairs from 6″-wide strips, see Cutting Wedges (page 13).

2. To piece a two-fabric 6″-wedge plate with a straight-edge finish, leave the pairs together as cut, and stack them in staggered pile RST with the *same fabric on top*. This ensures all pairs will be sewn along the same edge.

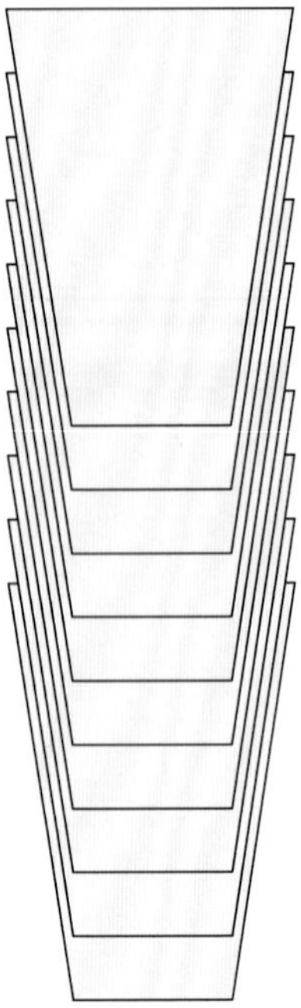

3. Chain piece wedge pairs together along the same long edge. Cut the wedges apart using a clipping tool (see Clipping Tool for Chain Piecing, page 72).

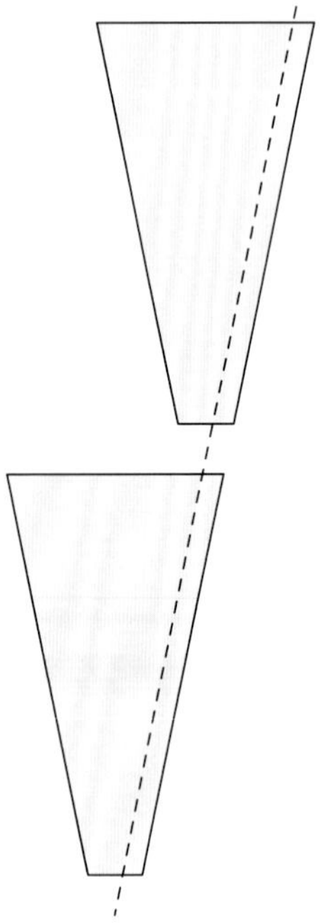

tip Use a ¼″ sewing machine presser foot with an edge to assist in seam width accuracy.

4. Press the seams open.

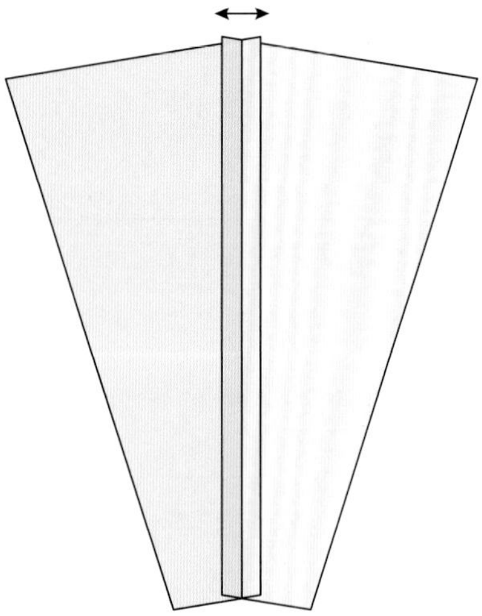

tip Using a pressing bar makes the open seams appear crisp and prevents pressing in wrong directions. For how to construct your own ham or pressing bar, see Pressing Bar (page 72).

5. Sew five-wedge pairs RST side to side to form a half-circle. Repeat with the remaining five pairs. Sew the half-circles together to form a complete circle. Press the seams open and press the block carefully.

6. Choose one of two methods—Method 1: Stay Stitching (below) or Method 2: Facing (page 20)—to finish the outside edge. The center is finished afterwards (see The Dresden Center, page 27).

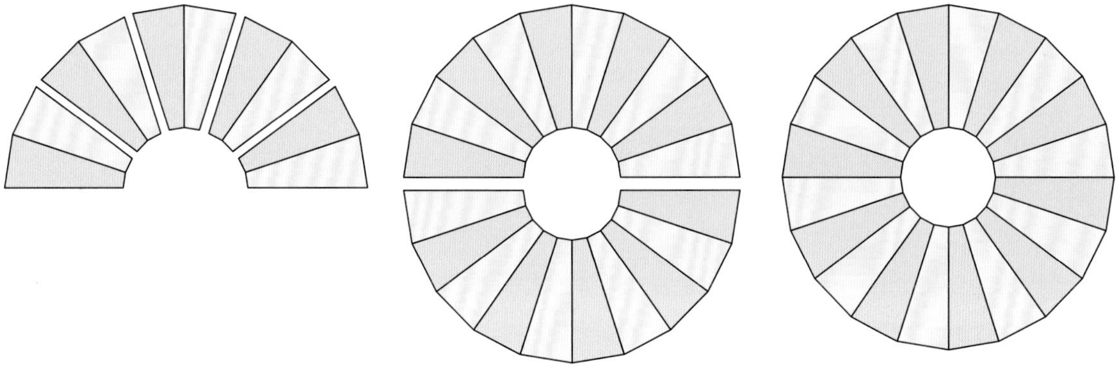

METHOD 1: STAY STITCHING

1. Sew completely around the plate, ¼″ inside the outer edge.

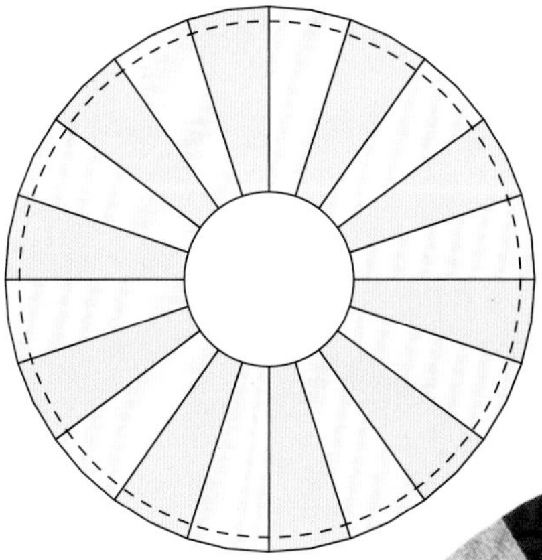

2. Carefully press the raw edge to the wrong side. Use the stitching as a guide to create a clean edge for appliquéing the block onto the background fabric.

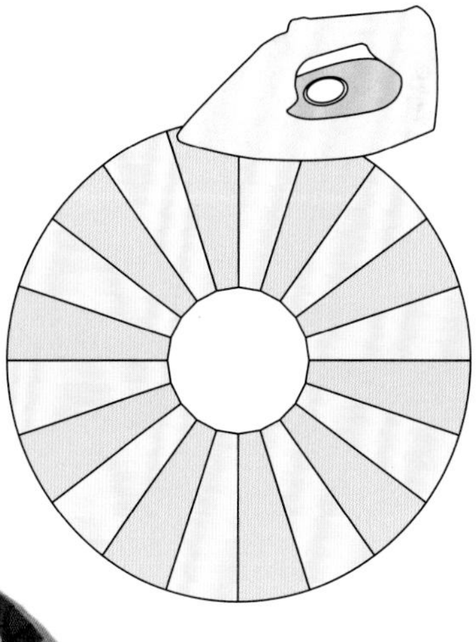

METHOD 2: FACING

1. Cut a piece of lightweight fusible interfacing slightly larger than the plate. *Do not cut it to the exact size.*

2. Pin the right side of the plate to the fusible or bumpy side of the interfacing. Stitch a ¼″ seam around the plate's outer edge.

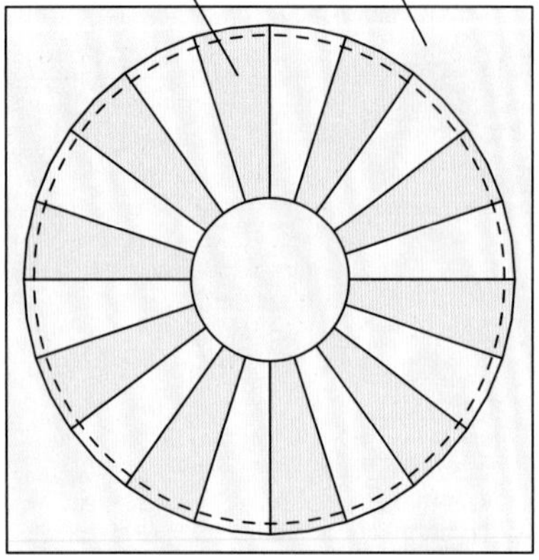

3. Trim away the extra fusible. Carefully cut an X in the interfacing only, without cutting the fabric.

4. Turn the plate right side out through the X. Use Alex Anderson's 4-in-1 Essential Sewing Tool (page 78) or a point turner to smooth out the curved edges to make a circle. Trim away the fusible from the center of the plate, leaving about a 2″ ring around the perimeter.

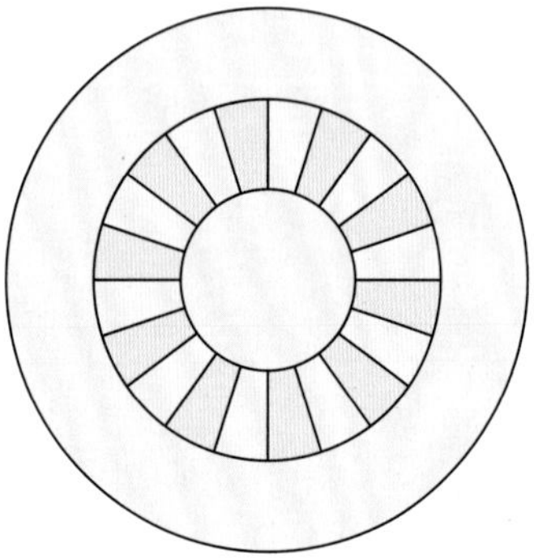

Back view after turning

5. Use a nonstick pressing sheet or a sheet of freezer paper to protect the ironing surface. Carefully press from the front of the plate. The fusible is now the back facing for the block. When appliquéing the block to a background, light ironing will fuse it in place to hold it for appliquéing.

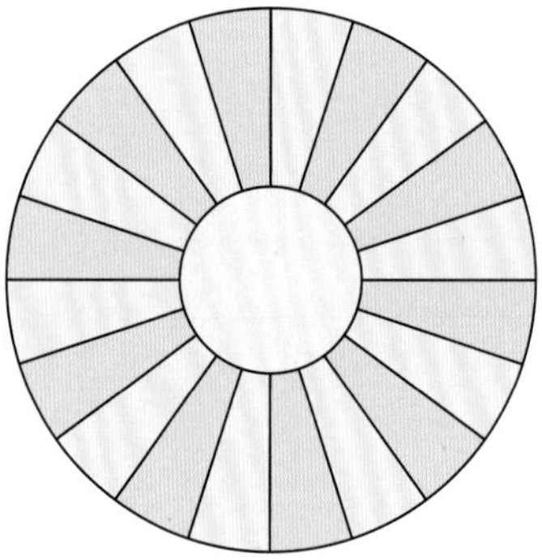

Front view

Pointed-Edge Plates

Ten-point Serendipity block

Twenty-point Dresden block

Pointed-edge plates are the mainstay of the Dresden blocks. They are constructed with ten or twenty points, and the pointed edges can be alternated with curved, straight, or three-sided edges. Both variations are wonderful for showcasing pieced techniques (see Dresden 201: Pieced Designs, page 34). These plates are especially attractive as a layer on top of a round straight-edge plate or another pointed block.

Note: Reverse Stitching Technique

Use the reverse stitching technique to join together any kind of wedges that have finished edges. To do this, start stitching ¼″ below the matched edges, reverse to the matched edges, then stitch forward to complete the entire seam. This secures the seams at the "valleys of each pair" and prevents having many small thread ends showing.

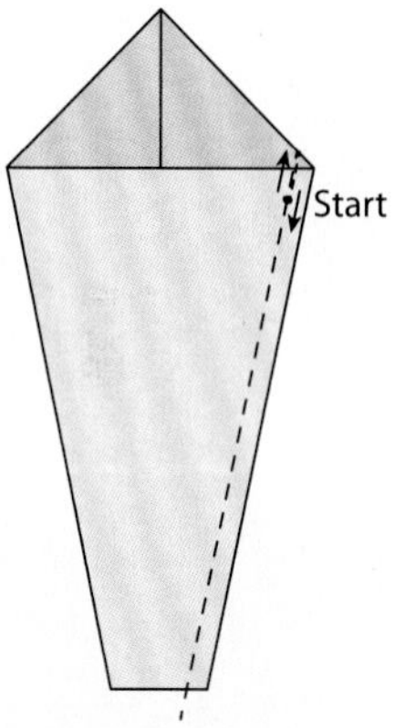

Reverse stitching technique to sew wedge pairs with finished edges

It is important to note that *all points are finished before* wedges are sewn into a circle. The twenty-point Dresden block is made with twenty individual wedges; the ten-point Serendipity Dresden is made with ten pairs of wedges.

Construction: Twenty-Point Plate

1. To cut twenty wedges from 6″-wide strips, refer to Cutting Wedges (page 13).

2. Fold each wedge lengthwise in half, RST, and stitch a ¼″ seam across the top edge.

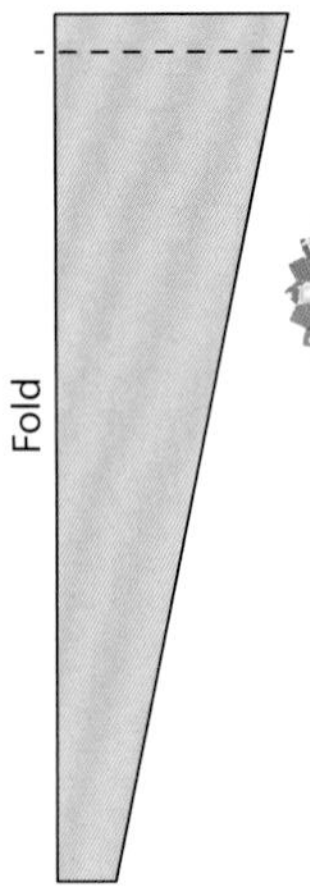

tip Use a shorter stitch length for more secure stitches. Chain piecing (page 71) makes the job easy.

3. Diagonally trim the corner of the sewn wedge at the fold to ease the bulk. Finger-press the seam open.

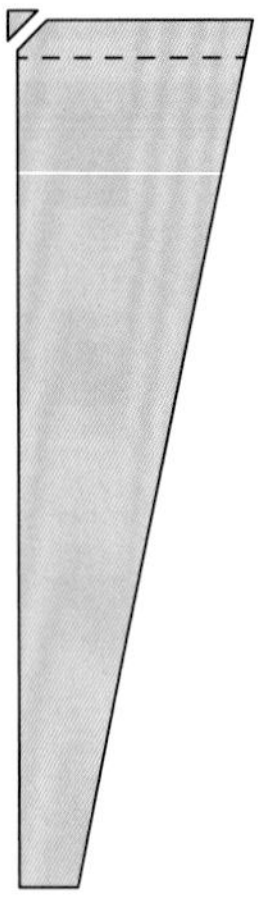

4. Turn the point to the right side. Use a turning tool to create a crisp point. Press carefully to avoid distortion and to ensure all points are symmetrical.

tip Create a tool for centering and pressing (see Centering Tool for Points, page 73) to keep your points symmetrical and crisp. Insert the tool into the back of the point, lining up your drawn line with the seamline, press.

5. Layout the wedges in pairs, lining up the folded edges RST. Stitch the pairs together, using the reverse stitching technique (page 21).

6. Join five pairs into half-circles and the half-circles to each other to create a plate.

Completed twenty-point Dresden

Construction: Serendipity Plate

The ten-point Serendipity block came about as the result of a mistake or rather a misdirection that produced a lovely point style. It is especially attractive as a flower or a star.

1. Follow Straight-Edge Plate, Construction, Steps 1–4 (page 18).

2. For each stitched pair refold the wedges RST. Sew across the top with a ¼″ seam allowance, keeping the previously sewn seam outward.

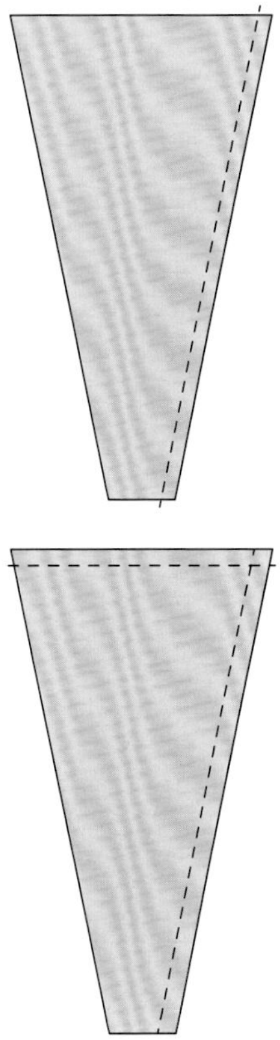

3. Diagonally trim at the fold, across the top, and the side to reduce bulk.

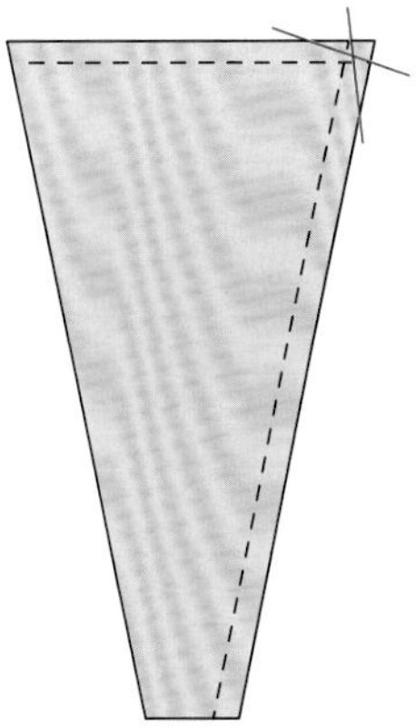

4. Finger-press the top seam open; gently turn and push out the point, using a turning tool. Make ten points.

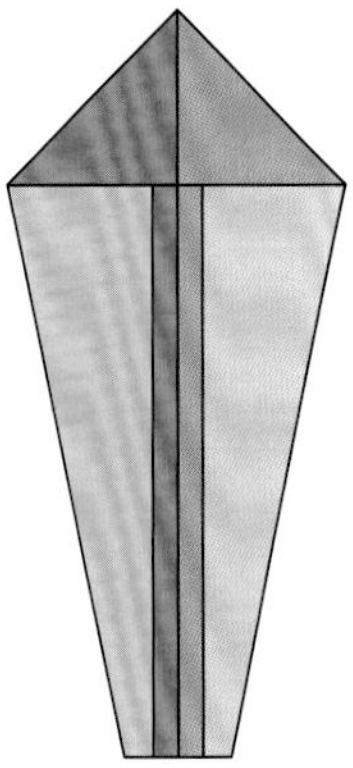

5. Sew the pairs together side to side, using the reverse stitching technique (page 21).

6. Press all the seams open.

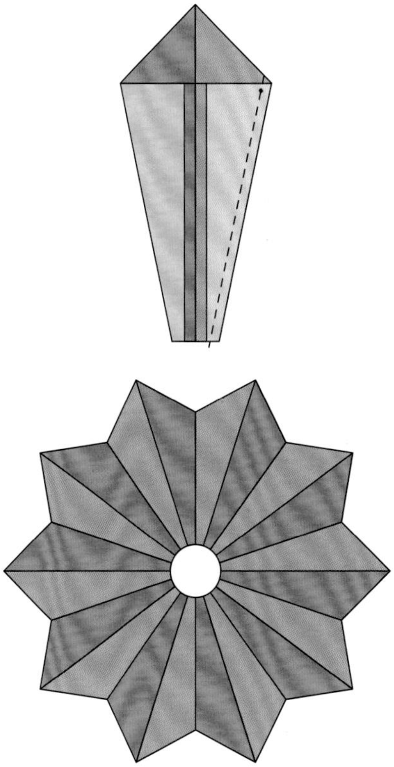

Curved-Edge Plate

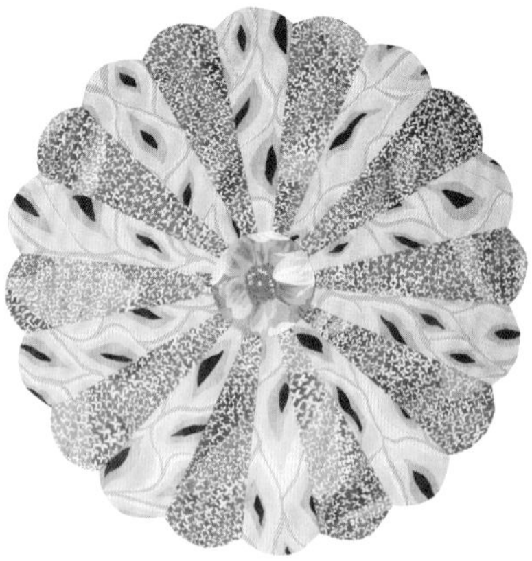

Curved edges are the most traditional edge finish of all the Dresden blocks. They are soft and lovely and can be combined with straight, pointed, or three-sided wedges within a single block. They can be a base layer or a second layer on top of another plate. The curves on 5″ wedges or larger tend to stand out a bit more.

All curved edges are faced before the wedges are sewn into a circle. Any circular object can be used to shape the curve at the wider top edge of the wedge. Mark a centerline on your circle template to line up with the wedge's fold. If you make the curve too deep, the seams will be difficult to line up and stitch.

Construction

1. To cut twenty wedges from 6″-wide strips, refer to Cutting Wedges, Steps 1–6 (page 13).

2. For the facings, cut twenty rectangles 2″ × 3½″ from muslin; matching fabric; or nonwoven, nonfusible interfacing.

3. Fold each wedge in half lengthwise, RST.

4. Use your circle template to mark and then cut a curved edge at the top of each wedge. If you are using a plastic or cardboard circle template, fold the template in half to mark the diameter. If you are using an acrylic circle template, you will find the centerlines are usually marked. Place the outside edge of the circle template at the top edge of the wedge and line up the centerline on the fold. Mark the curved edge. Cut with scissors or a small (28 mm) rotary cutter.

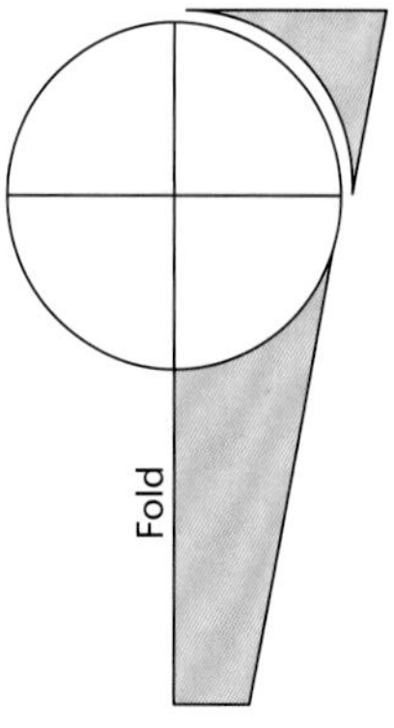

5. Open the wedge and place it RST on the facing rectangle. Stitch a scant ¼″ seam around the curve, keeping the seamline smooth.

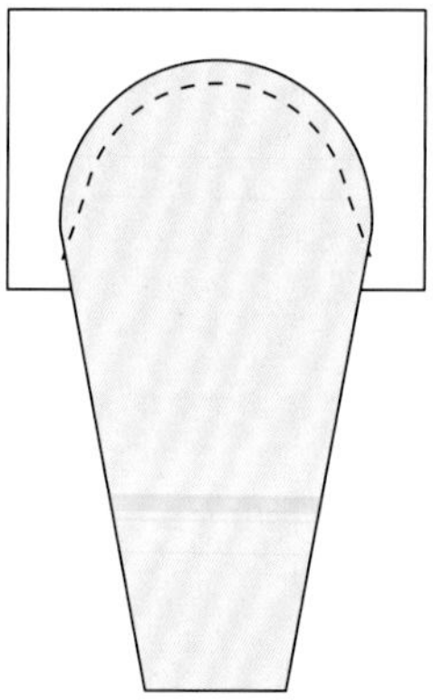

tip Shorten the stitch length slightly to ease the sewing of the curve.

6. Trim any excess facing along the top and sides of the wedge. Gently turn the piece right side out and press.

7. Complete the plate, sewing the wedges together using the reverse stitching technique (page 21).

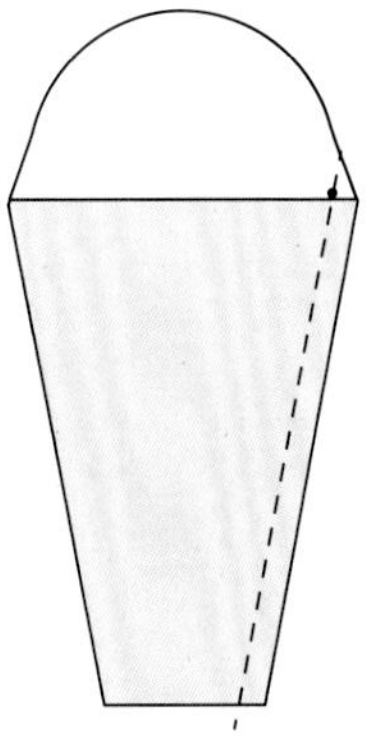

8. Press all the seams open

Three-Sided Edge Plate

The three-sided wedge plate has a dramatic petal appearance and can be alternated with curved or pointed-edge wedges. These plates stand out alone or as the bottom layer of two plates. Similar to the curved edge, a facing is used to complete the edge before sewing the plate together.

Construction

1. Follow Curved-Edge Plate, Construction, Steps 1–3 (page 24).

2. Lay the 60° line of a ruler along the top edge of the wedge and ½″ away from the fold.

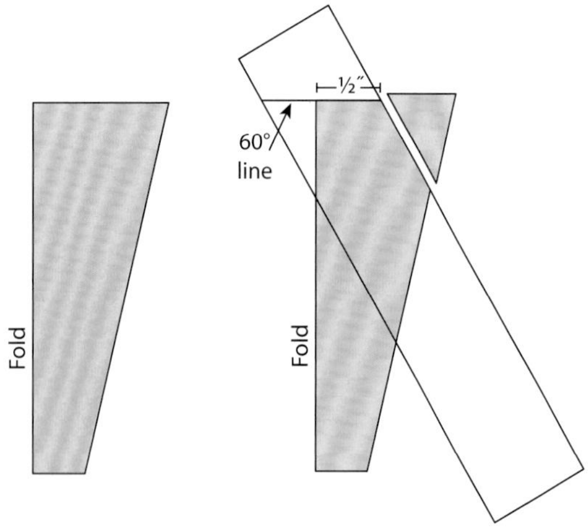

3. Trim away the *nonfolded* edge with a rotary cutter.

4. Open the wedge and place it RST on the facing rectangle. Sew the top three sides with a ¼″ seam.

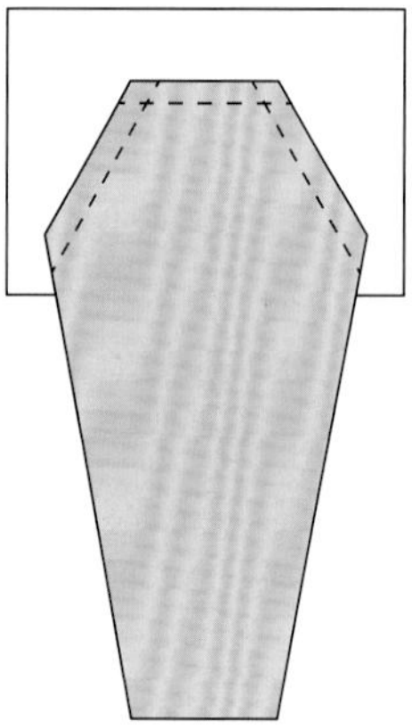

5. Trim the excess facing and corners. Turn and gently push out the points using a turning tool.

6. Complete the plate by sewing wedges together, using the reverse stitching technique (page 21).

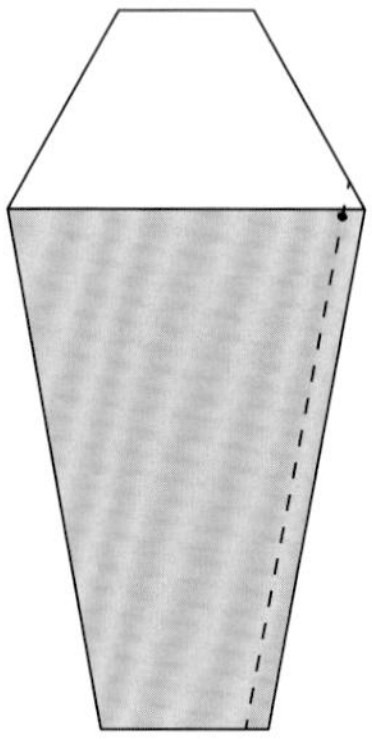

7. Press all the seams open.

The Dresden Center

At this stage with your plates created, you might think that it's time to appliqué them to a background. However, left as they are, these blocks will easily distort as you work to arrange them or secure them to backgrounds. The next step will be to stabilize the center opening. This will ensure the plates maintain a uniform shape.

Stabilize the Center Opening

Stabilizing the center opening is an important step and is done for all plates.

1. Measure the center opening of the plate and cut a piece of fusible interfacing (such as Pellon 906F) ½″ larger.

2. Use a nonstick pressing sheet or a sheet of freezer paper to protect the ironing surface. Lay the plate facedown on the pressing sheet and line up the fusible interfacing with the center opening, bumpy side down; fuse. This prevents the plate from warping as you stitch the center on. The exposed fusible in the center can also be used to "hold" the finished center while it is stitched in place.

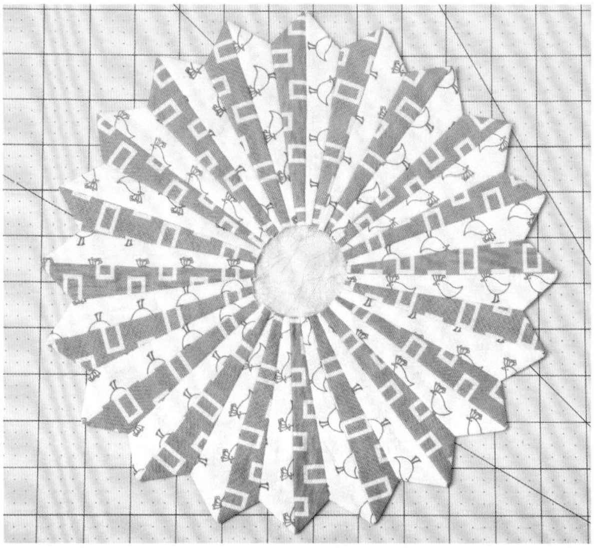

Stabilized center opening

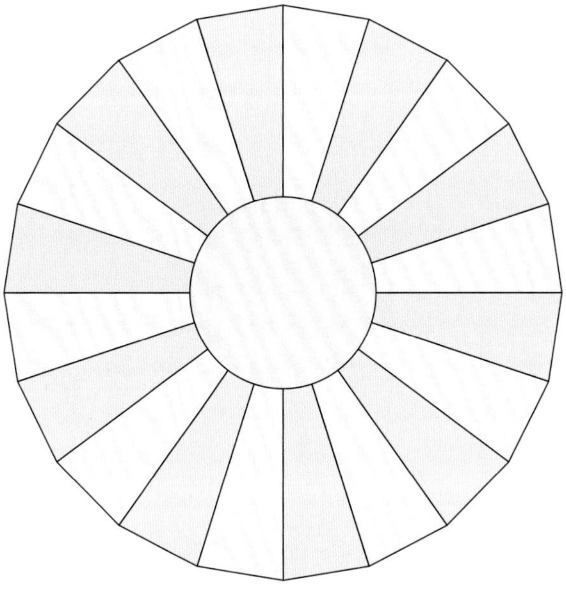

Fusible interfacing stabilizing center

Make the Center

Now that the plate is stabilized, our attention is focused on the unfinished edges at the center of the block that remain. Consider first whether your project will involve layering different blocks on top of each other. If plates are layered, only the ones whose centers are exposed require a center treatment. For the plates that need it, fabric centers finish the plates and hide the narrow ends of the wedges. They are made from 3″–5″ circles, squares, triangles, or hexagons and may be single- or multilayered. You can use the 3″ and 3½″ circle template patterns (page 77).

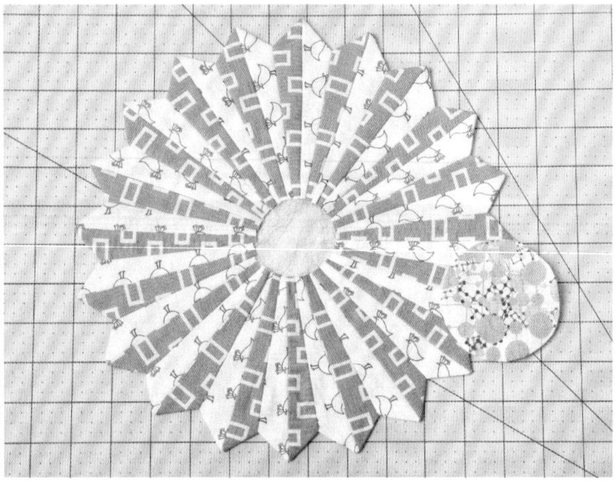

There are a few things to keep in mind when planning a center treatment for any plate.

- Centers provide the perfect opportunity to fussy cut from a special fabric to really pop the look of a plate.
- Don't feel like you must use the same fabrics you used for the wedges. Add something new.
- Centers are traditionally circular but can be square, hexagonal, triangular, layered, or any shape you wish.
- As for size, they need to cover the center opening by at least ¼″ on all sides.
- Centers are added only to the top plate in a stack.
- There are several ways to create centers, such as with freezer paper, plastic templates, or facings.
- Use a placement tool to position the center exactly in the middle of a plate. They are easy to make (refer to the instructions in Center Placement Tool, page 73).

Using Freezer Paper

Fabric to fussy cut for the center

Depending on the size of the plate, a Dresden's center opening can range in size between 2½″ to 3″ diameter or more. Remember the center will need to finish ½″ larger than the opening to have room to overlap the plate. Add a ½″ to the opening's size to arrive at your *desired center size.*

1. Cut two pieces of freezer paper into rough circles about ½″ or more larger than the *desired center size.* Press both pieces together, paper sides up, to make a stiffer template.

2. Use a template pattern (page 77) or a die cutter to cut the desired size circle from the freezer paper sandwich.

3. Press the waxy side of the freezer paper to the wrong side of the chosen fabric.

4. Rough cut the fabric, leaving a generous ¼″ seam allowance around the freezer paper.

5. Sew a basting stitch by hand or machine in the seam allowance around the freezer paper.

6. Pull the basting thread gently to take in seam allowance and bring in the edges of the fabric around the freezer-paper template.

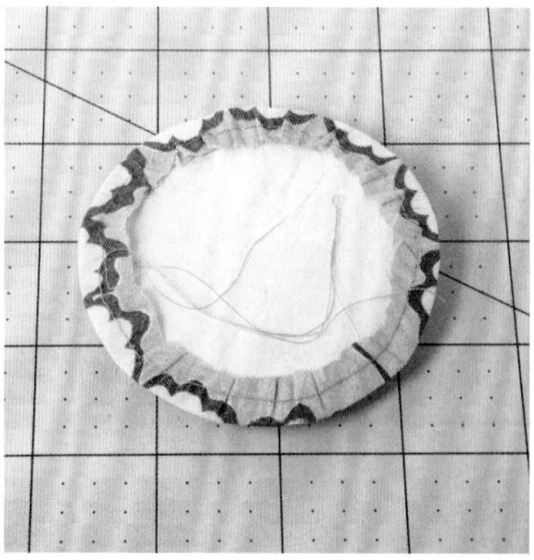

7. Spray the circle with starch and press. Remove the freezer paper once the circle is cool. Now the circle is ready to attach to the plate.

8. Use the center placement tool (page 73) to position the circle onto the right side of the plate. Whipstitch the turned edge by hand or use an invisible machine stitch to secure the circle to the plate.

Center placed on block

Hand stitched center

Using a Facing

Lightweight fabrics; nonfusible, nonwoven interfacing; or muslin can be used to make a facing for the centers. These options are helpful when a specific motif is desired because they are transparent enough to allow for the desired placement.

1. Decide on the center size and shape and roughly cut out the facing material larger than the desired center. Use a fabric-safe marker or mechanical pencil to draw the desired shape onto the facing material.

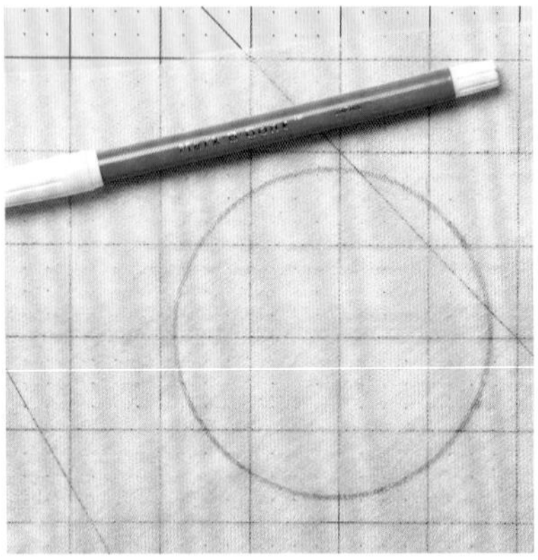

2. Place the facing and center fabric RST and stitch on the drawn line.

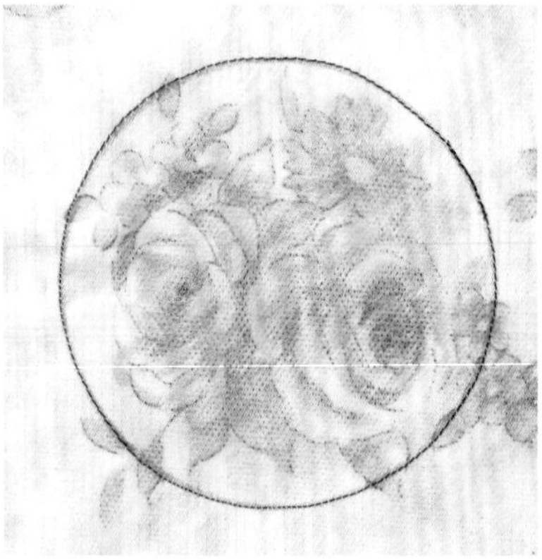

3. Trim both layers a scant ¼″ around the stitched line.

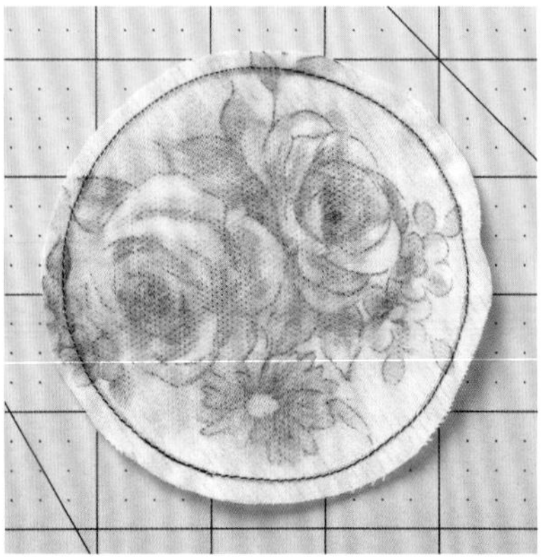

4. Cut a small X in the facing material, being careful not to cut the center fabric.

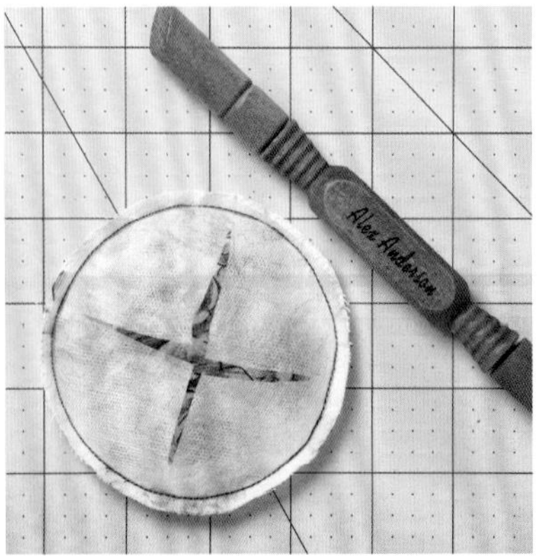

5. Turn the center right side out through the X in the facing, gently pushing into shape and smoothing the edges. Spray starch and press the circle.

6. Use the center placement tool (page 73) to position the circle onto the right side of the plate. Whipstitch the turned edge by hand or use an invisible machine stitch to secure the circle to the plate.

Dresden Block Edges: Construction Steps

The following construction flow chart is a visual roadmap for making the various kinds of Dresden block edges.

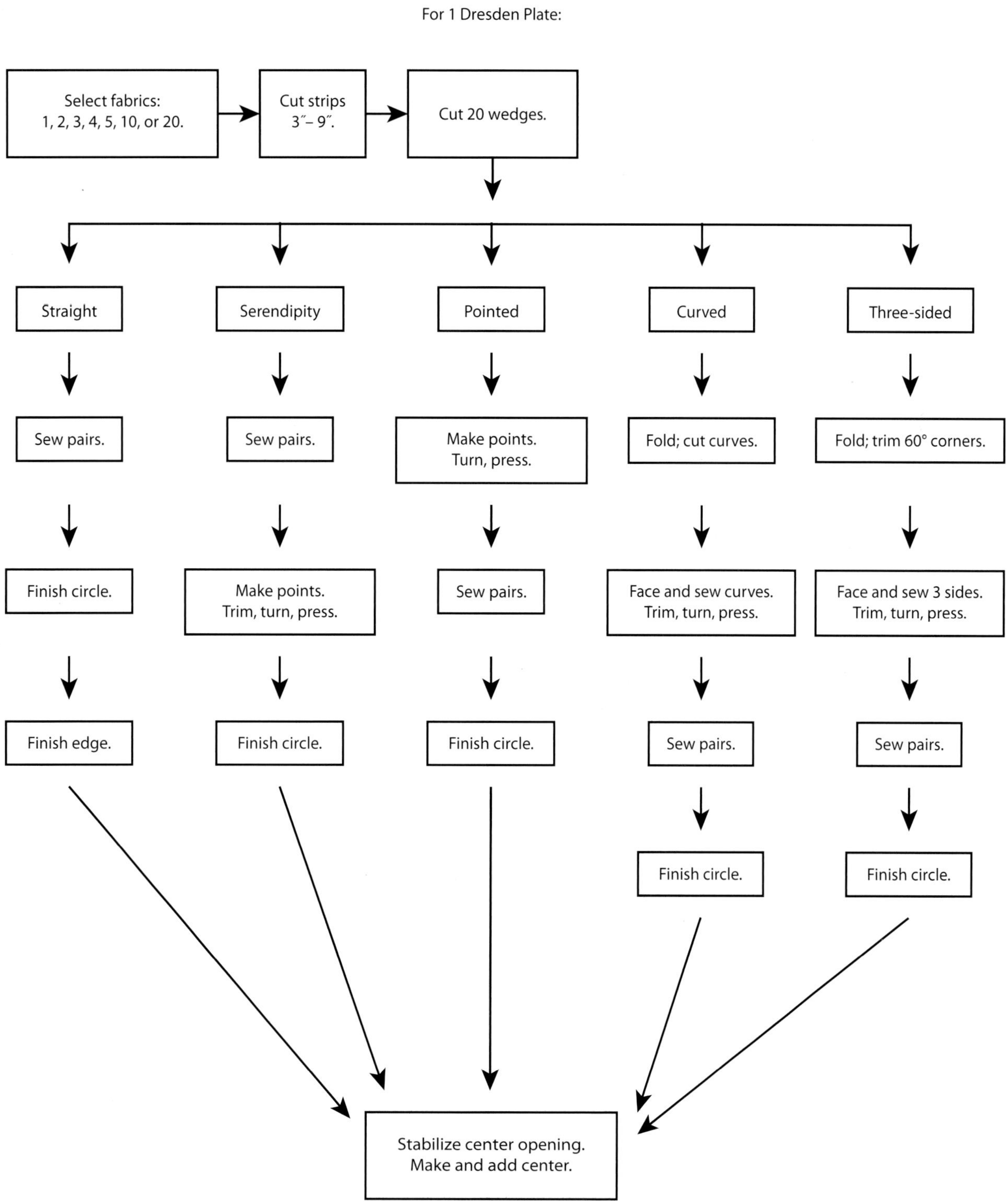

Putting It All Together

Now that you know how to make the plates, you might ask how many you should make and just what to do with your beautiful Dresden blocks? I recommend first making several blocks in your favorite fabrics. Decide afterwards how to use them. A traditional quilt, an art quilt, a baby quilt, a wallhanging, or even a pillow are a few of the choices. Pick your background fabrics after you have made several plates, and be sure to make plates in multiple sizes with a variety of edge finishes. Regardless the type or size of the background for your finished plates, use a design wall to lay them out to help determine your background size. Try several different background colors or use multiple fabrics pieced together.

A Traditional Setting

Appliqué each plate to a background block and sew the blocks together into a traditionally set quilt. You can choose a row by row or on-point setting, with or without sashings, borders, or cornerstones. To find blocks and their corresponding background sizes, consult the Plate Sizes and Traditional Backgrounds chart (page 14).

An "Art Quilt"

By definition, a Dresden plate "art quilt" is a group of plates appliquéd in a random manner to a background fabric. The background can be one solid fabric or pieced with several fabrics, as shown in quilts in the Gallery (page 62). If you decide to make a large bed-size art quilt, first determine your layout on the background. Lay the plates out in an S-shape and then fill in. Don't be afraid to overlap and layer. Do you want the plates to touch the edges or remain in the middle of the quilt? Maybe some plates need to be trimmed to partial plates at the quilt's edge. Look for ideas and inspiration in the Gallery. Give yourself plenty of time to move the plates around before deciding on a final layout. Take photos with a camera or a smartphone to record your layouts and evaluate them for value. Turn on the black-and-white filter to better help you read your value arrangement.

Preparing the Background

I usually quilt my backgrounds first and then add the plates. I tend to quilt the background in a very simple allover pattern. After the plates are appliquéd in place, it's time to quilt the plates. If the quilt is large, consider dividing the background into sections to make it easier to handle as you appliqué the plates in place. Save some of the plates to appliqué over the seamlines once the background is pieced. This makes it easier to finish the final quilting on just the plates.

Attaching Plates to the Background

You can secure the plates to the background in one of three ways:

Appliqué by hand: Appliqué the plates to the background by hand with a simple whipstitch, using a matching thread color. I recommend using a small amount of fusible (such as Mistyfuse) or fabric glue to hold the plate in place while you sew it down. This helps avoid being "stuck" by multiple pins and keeps the plate from shifting. Remember the straight-edge plates already have the fusible in place!

Appliqué by machine: The plates can also be appliquéd by machine, using a straight, overlock, or blanket stitch. This works well on small quilts because this method requires a lot of maneuvering of the quilt top under the throat of the sewing machine. Again, secure the plates to the background with glue or fusible first.

Quilted: The plates can also be quilted down. Prepare the quilt sandwich and quilt the background first with a simple all over design. Position the plates with safety pins, fusible interfacing or glue, and then quilt the plates. Different fun designs can be quilted on each plate. I find this method much easier than quilting around all the small areas of each plate.

Quilting the Plates

There are several ways to quilt the plates once they are attached to the background, and to show them off!

- Use a design in the fabric and repeat it over the entire plate.
- Quilt the plate as one big flower.
- Quilt each wedge in a repetitive design.

DRESDEN 201:
pieced designs

Having learned the different edge treatments and finishes for the Dresden plate blocks, now is the time to jazz them up with extra piecing, fabric combinations, and color arrangements. In this section, we will look at piecing the individual wedges. There are several ways of piecing and cutting the wedges to achieve the unique looks of these more sophisticated Dresdens. The Split-Wedge, Bull's-Eye, Sawtooth, Cogwheel, and Flying Geese blocks are just some of the more advanced pieced-wedge styles that can be made into plates.

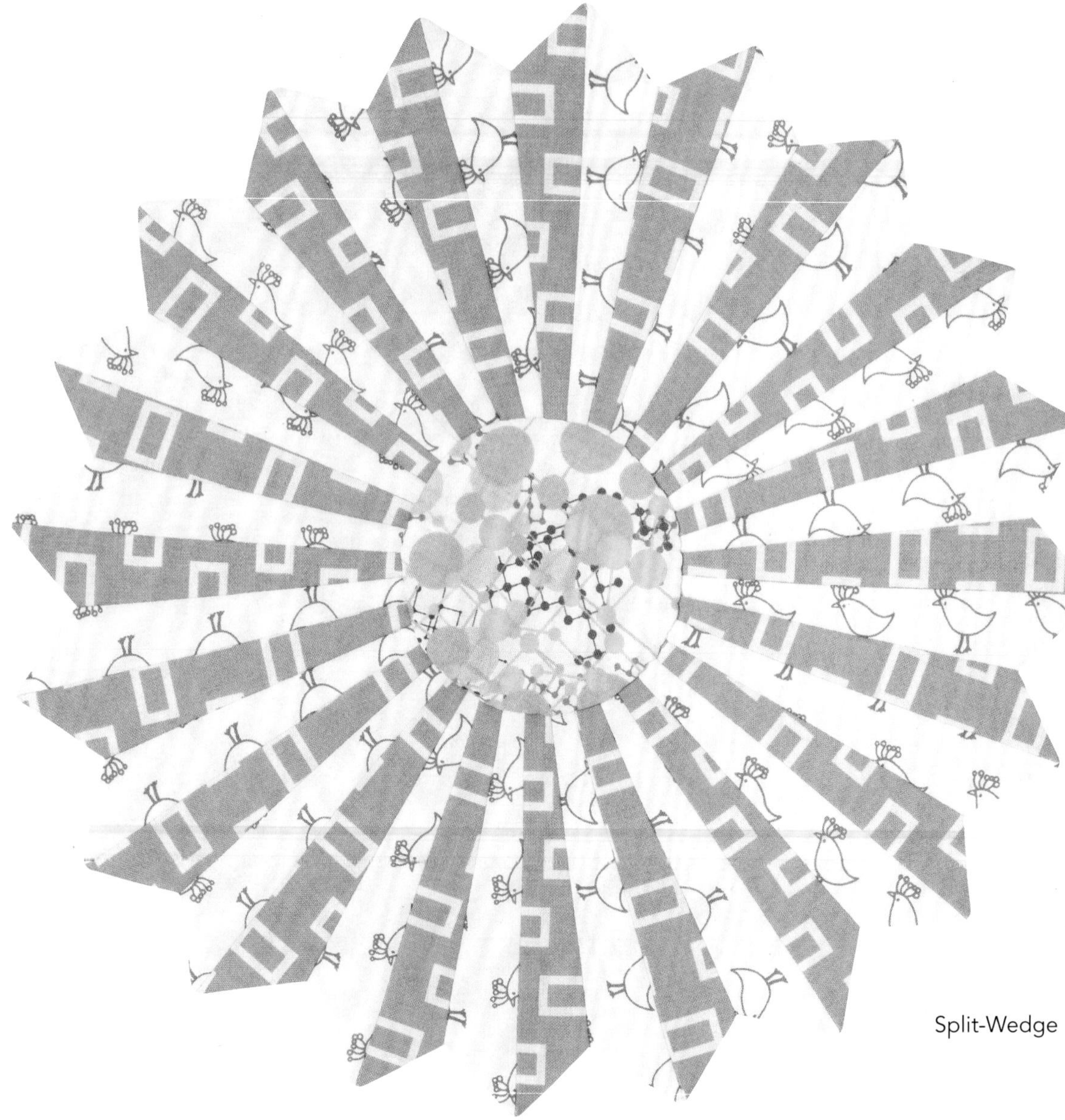

Split-Wedge

Strip-Set Piecing

Creating the most basic pieced-wedge plate starts with a strip set. You may already be familiar with strip sets when piecing Four- or Nine-Patch blocks. The concept is simple. Cut a WOF strip from at least two different fabrics. Sew them together lengthwise to make a strip set and subcut sections from the strip. In the case of the Dresden plate, the subcut is the wedge shape, which we learned to cut previously from strips in Cutting Wedges (page 13).

Note: Heads Up!

Cutting wedges from single layers of fabric or from pieced strip sets … What's the difference? With single fabrics you have the option of layering strips. Layering and cutting produces pairs of wedges. When cutting from pieced strip sets, wedges are cut one at a time for greatest accuracy.

Most pieced wedges can be categorized as either **symmetric** or **asymmetric**. These terms refer to the *width* of the strips within a strip set. When all the strips are the same width, the strip set and the wedge cut from it are symmetric. However, if the strips are cut at *varying widths*, the strip set and the wedge cut from it are asymmetric. Working with the concepts of symmetric and asymmetric Dresdens is the launching point into the realm of pieced designs.

Using the pieced strip-set method of making Dresden wedges will inherently have a secondary consequence that should be considered. Namely, that wedges in two distinct colorways will emerge. The fabrics are the same, but the order of their appearance has changed. The constant flipping of the ruler while cutting strip sets allows for the fabric to appear in reverse order every second wedge. To achieve the stunning visual effects this design method offers, the wedges will need to be separated into two sets of different colorways after cutting from a pieced strip set.

For both symmetric- and asymmetric-pieced blocks, wedge size is best 6″–9″. Given the size range for wedges, it follows that symmetric wedges are made from only two or three different fabric strips of the same width. Asymmetric-pieced blocks, on the other hand, are capable of featuring two, three, or four fabrics cut in different strip widths. Plan your wedge size first; then determine how many fabrics you want to use in the strip set and go for it!

Once your pieced wedges have been created, the choice of the finished edge and block center will further add to the unique quality of your blocks. The possibilities are endless!

tip Asymmetric and symmetric blocks can be made with an additional single-fabric wedge that alternates between the pieced wedges. Cutting twenty wedges of each—pieced and single-fabric—will result in *two unique blocks*! (See Adding Single-Fabric Wedges, page 43.)

Symmetric-Pieced Wedges

Symmetric blocks

By definition the symmetric wedge will have strips of fabric the same width pieced together lengthwise. The result of sewing symmetric wedges together is the horizontal seams of each wedge will meet at each juncture. To a quilter, this is the time to "nest your seams." For this reason, the seams of symmetric-pieced strip sets will always be pressed to *one* side. They will naturally nest, or lock together, when wedges of the second colorway are turned upright and slotted between wedges of the first colorway. The horizontal seams will run unbroken around the plate, giving the appearance of two circles within each plate with perfectly offset fabrics.

Note

The larger the wedge, the greater the chances are that two or more strip sets will be needed in order to make all twenty wedges. The "Strip Sets" column in the charts in this chapter will let you know when that is the case.

Symmetric Wedges: Two Fabrics

This is a good block to make when you want to use a certain fabric motif or design.

1. Select two fabrics and decide the wedge size you want.

2. Refer to the Cutting Symmetric Two-Fabric Wedges chart (next page) for the strip size and the number of strips needed for each fabric.

3. Cut the necessary size WOF strips from each fabric.

4. Piece the fabrics into a strip set; press the seam to *one side*. Make another strip set whenever multiple strips are called for. Multiple strip sets may be required to cut all twenty wedges.

5. Cut twenty individual wedges, using the ruler technique described in Cutting Wedges (page 13).

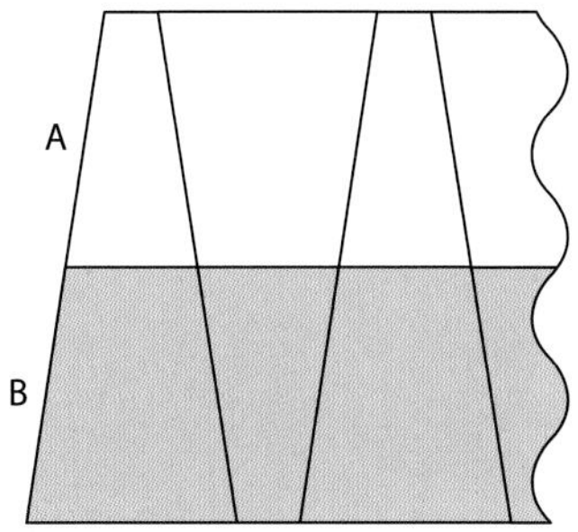

6. Separate wedges into two sets by colorway and follow Construction: Pieced Symmetric Wedges (page 38), to complete the plate.

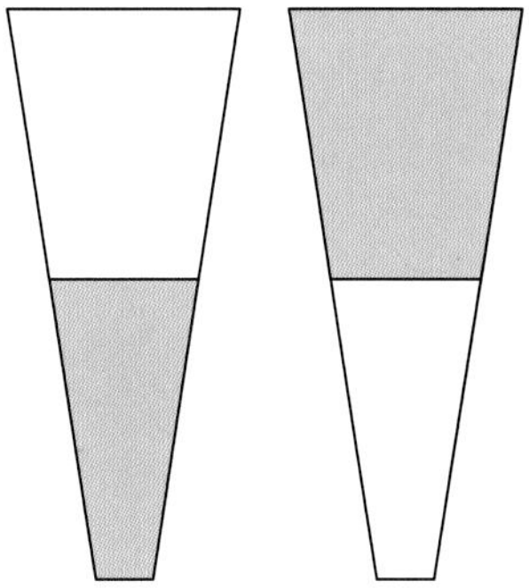

CUTTING SYMMETRIC TWO-FABRIC WEDGES

Wedge size	Fabrics A and B	
	Strip width	Strip sets
6″	3¼″	1
7″	3¾″	1
8″	4¼″	1
9″	4¾″	2

Symmetric Wedges: Three Fabrics

Symmetric three-fabric plates are characterized by a distinct banding effect created by the second fabric in the strip set. Use value in your fabric choices to give the illusion of circles radiating from the center outward.

1. Select three fabrics and decide the wedge size you want.

2. Refer to the Cutting Symmetric Three-Fabric Wedges chart (at right) for the strip size and the number of strips needed for each fabric.

3. Follow Symmetric Wedges: Two Fabrics, Steps 3–6 (previous page).

CUTTING SYMMETRIC THREE-FABRIC WEDGES

Wedge size	Fabrics A, B, and C	
	Strip width	Strip sets
6″	2⅜″	1
6½″	2½″	1
7″	2⅝″	1
8″	3″	1
9″	3⅜″	2

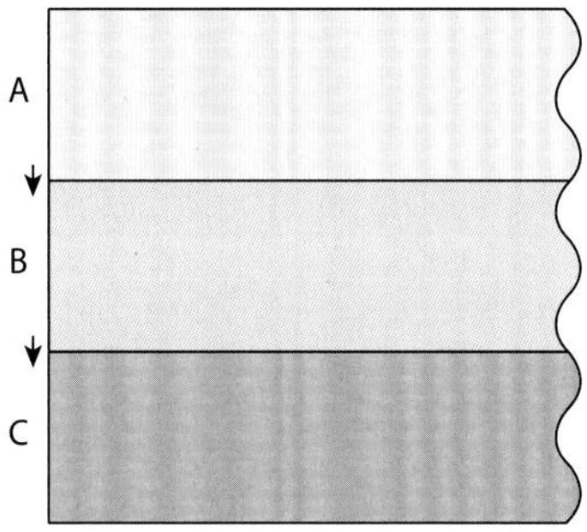

Symmetric three-fabric strip set

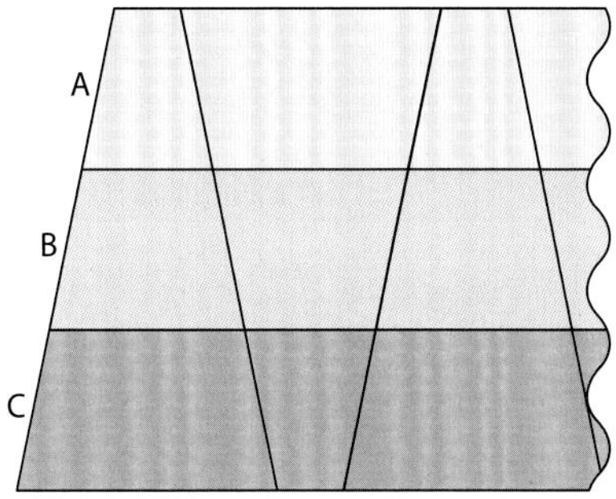

Cut the wedges.

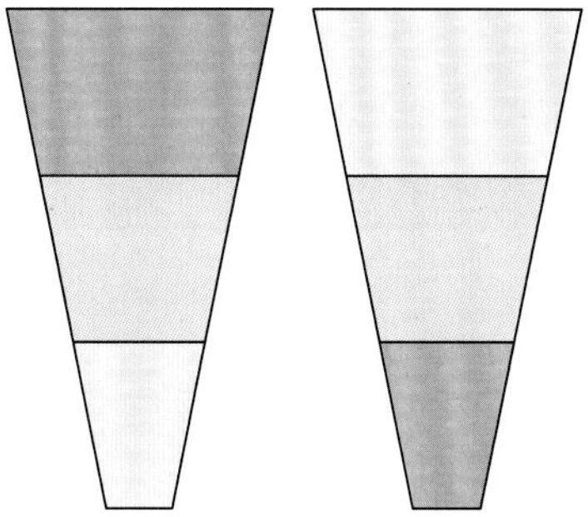
Two colorways of symmetric three-fabric wedges

Construction: Pieced Symmetric Wedges

1. Prepare the wedges with the desired edge finish (see Edge Variations, page 17).

Note: *If a straight-edge plate is desired,* continue to Steps 2–4. Before completing the center, choose either Method 1: Stay Stitching (page 19) or Method 2: Facing (page 20) to finish the edge.

2. Match a wedge from one colorway to another wedge in the second colorway RST. Nest the seams and pin. All pairs should have a wedge of the same colorway on top to ensure the same side seam is sewn consistently for all pairs.

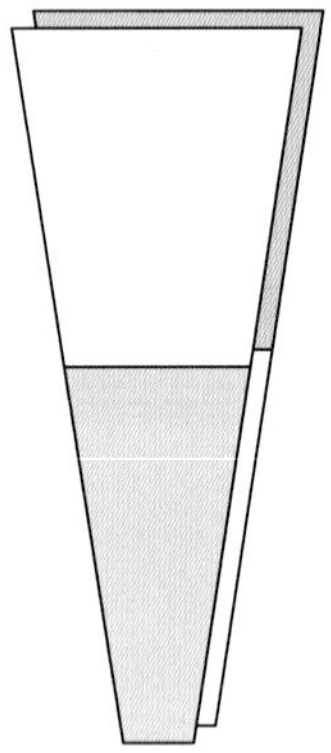

Two-fabric, two-colorway pair

3. Sew the ten pairs together using the reverse stitching technique (page 21). Press the seams.

4. Join five pairs into half-circles and then half-circles to each other to create a plate. Complete the center (see The Dresden Center, page 27).

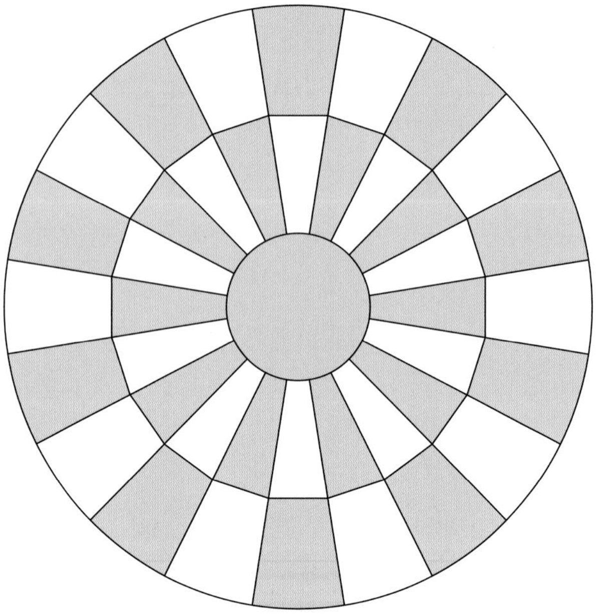

Symmetric two-fabric plate

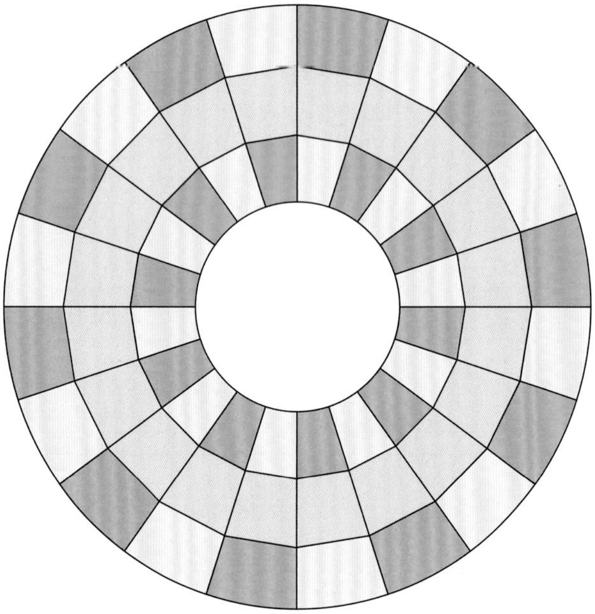

Symmetric three-fabric plate

Asymmetric-Pieced Wedges

Asymmetric two-fabric Dresden:
Cogwheel

Asymmetric four-fabric Dresden:
Bull's-Eye

Asymmetric Wedges: Two Fabrics

An asymmetric Dresden has two fabrics of unequal widths that make up the wedge. These plates lend themselves well to improvisational piecing and may speak to your style of block creation! For our purposes we will explore the very distinct design of an asymmetric two-fabric Dresden: the Cogwheel.

COGWHEEL DRESDEN

The Cogwheel Dresden is a unique style of an asymmetric two-fabric plate that has a decidedly Steampunk appearance. Its signature feature is that two pieced strip sets must be configured with the same fabrics but in opposite positions. The resulting wedges in four colorways are reconfigured into two blocks of opposite color layouts. It is particularly dramatic when a print and a solid comprise the strip sets. An added benefit is that you always finish with two blocks. The Cogwheel is suitable for any edge finish; however, the straight-edge finish has a more wheel-like appearance. Wedge size varies 6″–9″.

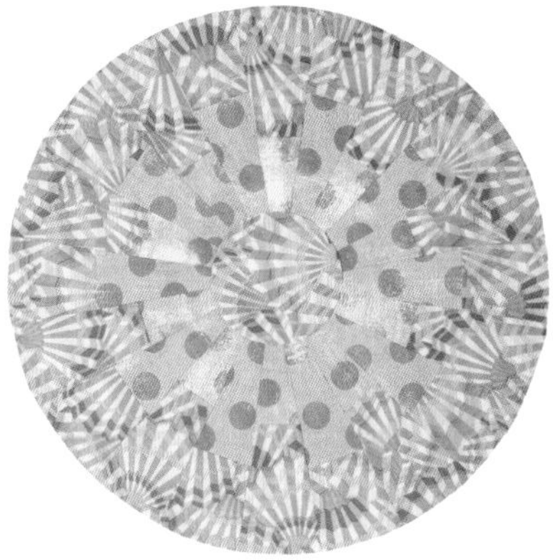

CUTTING COGWHEEL WEDGES

The number of strip sets required will make two unique plates.

Wedge size	Fabrics A and B		
	Strip width		Strip sets
	Narrow	Wide	
6″	2¾″	3¾″	2
7″	3¼″	4¼″	2
8″	3¾″	4¾″	2
9″	4¼″	5¼″	2

Construction

1. Select two contrasting fabrics.

2. Refer to the Cutting Cogwheel Wedges chart (at left) and cut a narrow and wide strip of each Fabric A and B, according to the desired wedge size.

3. Piece two strip sets as follows: narrow A to wide B; wide A to narrow B. Press the seams.

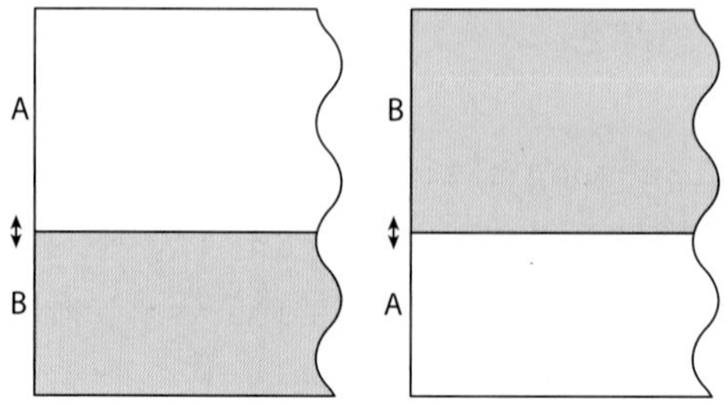

4. Cut twenty wedges from each strip set, using the ruler technique in Cutting Wedges (page 13).

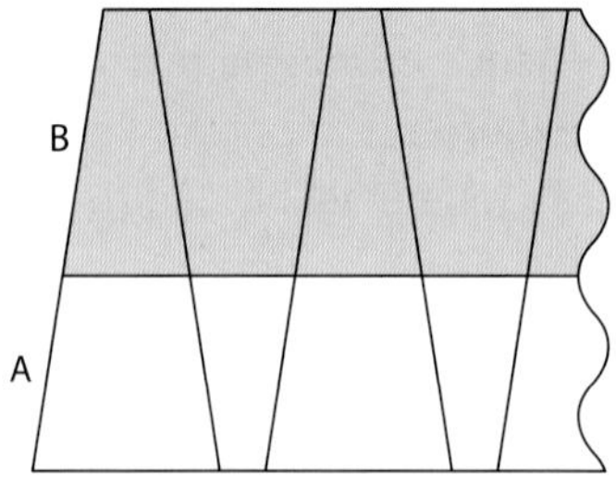

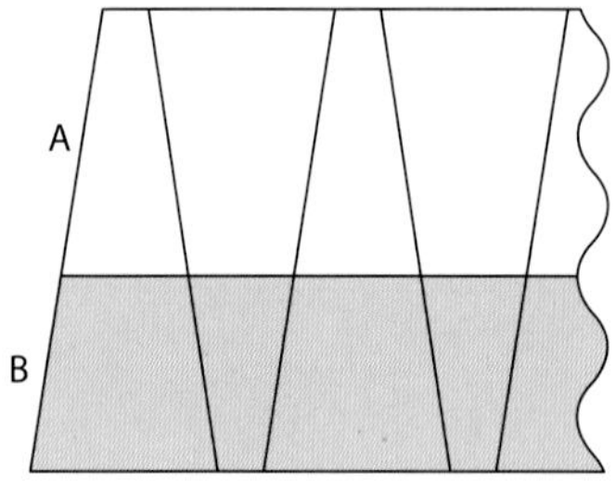

5. Sort the wedges into four sets of colorways, ten wedges per set. Two sets will have Fabric A at the narrow end of the wedges and two sets will have Fabric B at the narrow end.

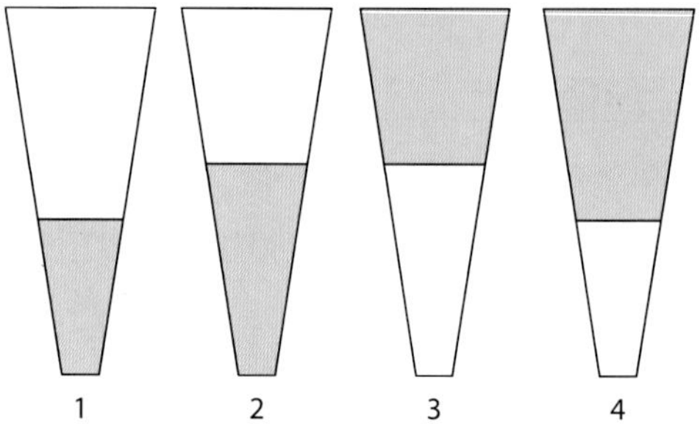

Sorted wedges

6. Use sets 1 and 2 to make Cogwheel Dresden 1; and sets 3 and 4 to make Cogwheel Dresden 2.

7. Continue with Asymmetric Wedges: Four Fabrics, Steps 1–4 (next page).

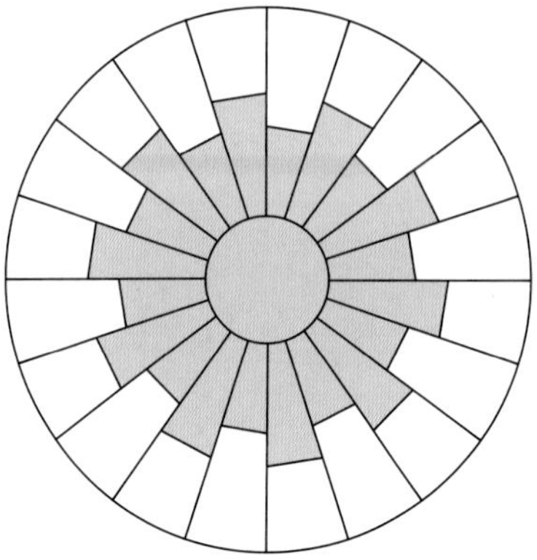

Cogwheel Dresden 1

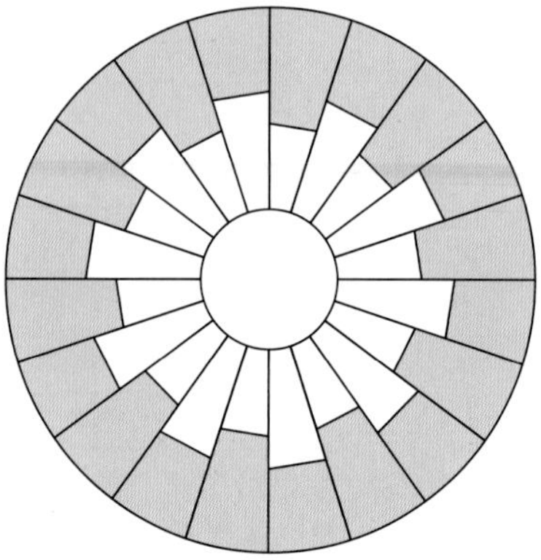

Cogwheel Dresden 2

Asymmetric Wedges: Four Fabrics

We worked out the math for you to create an asymmetric plate with four strips of varying widths!

1. Select four fabrics with light and dark contrasts. Determine the wedge size.

2. Cut WOF strips according to the Cutting Asymmetric Four-Fabric Wedges chart (below) for each of the four fabrics.

3. Sew strips together into an A-B-C-D sequence. Note that larger wedge sizes may require extra strip sets. Press seams open.

4. Cut twenty wedges from the strip set.

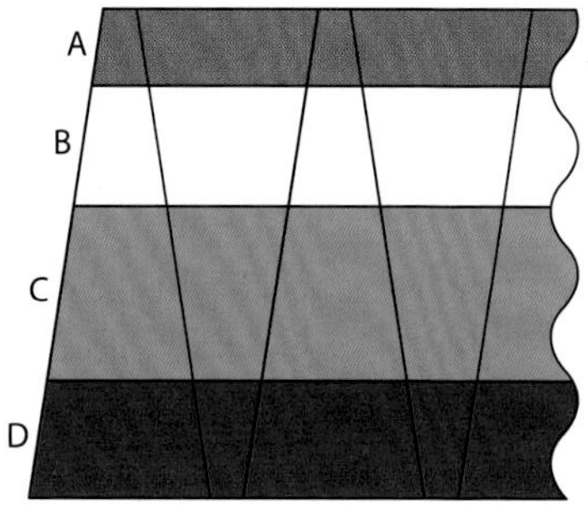

5. Separate the wedges into two sets by colorway.

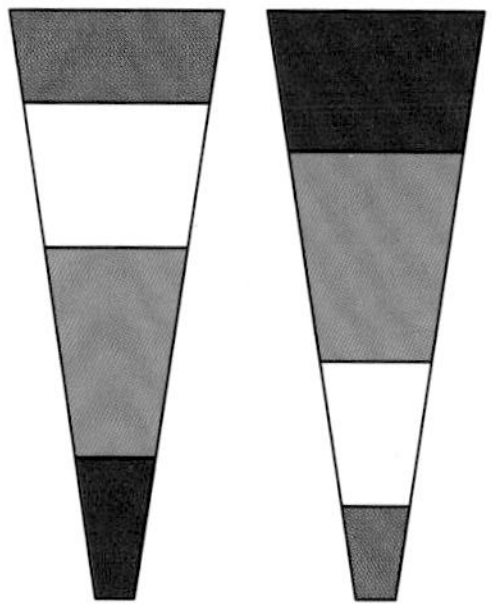

CUTTING ASYMMETRIC FOUR-FABRIC WEDGES

Wedge size	Strip width				Strip sets
	Fabric A	Fabric B	Fabric C	Fabric D	
6″	1¼″	2¼″	2½″	1½″	1
7″	1½″	2½″	2¾″	1¾″	1
8″	1½″	3″	2¾″	2¼″	1
8½″	2″	3¼″	2¾″	2″	2
9″	2¼″	3¼″	3″	2″	2

Construction

1. Prepare the wedges with the desired edge finishes (see Edge Variations, page 17).

Note: *If a straight-edge plate is desired*, continue to Steps 2–4. Before completing the center, choose either Method 1: Stay Stitching (page 19) or Method 2: Facing (page 20) to finish the edge.

2. Select a wedge from each colorway and pair RST. All ten pairs should have a wedge of the same colorway on top.

3. Sew the ten pairs together using the reverse stitching technique (page 21). Press the seams.

4. Join five pairs into half-circles and then half-circles to each other to make a plate. Complete the center (see The Dresden Center, page 27).

BULL'S-EYE DRESDEN

The Bull's-Eye Dresden is a unique variation of an asymmetric four-fabric plate constructed according to a specific design formula. It may look complicated, but it's all about the fabric choices. Generally, a Bull's-Eye consists of one or two solid fabrics of which one can be a fabric that reads like a solid. The solids are slotted specifically as Fabrics B and D in the strip-set sequence. This formula creates an illusion that naturally moves the eye in a circular rotation around the block. Careful fabric selection creates depth in your design and the rotational effect as well. It is a dramatic block and often forms the centerpiece of a decorative project.

Wedge size for this block can be 7″–9″. Any edge finish works well.

Bull's-Eye Dresden

CUTTING BULL'S-EYE DRESDENS

Wedge size	Strip width				Strip sets
	Fabric A: Print	Fabric B: Solid	Fabric C: Light print	Fabric D: Solid	
7″	3″	1¼″	2¼″	2″	1
8″	3½″	1¼″	2½″	2¼″	2
9″	3¾″	1½″	2¾″	2½″	2

Construction

1. Select four fabrics: (A) print, (B) solid, (C) light print, and (D) solid or a fabric that reads as a solid.

2. Refer to the Cutting Bull's-Eye Dresdens chart (above) and cut the WOF strips required for the wedge size desired.

3. Piece the fabrics into the required number of strip sets, following the A-B-C-D order. Press the seams.

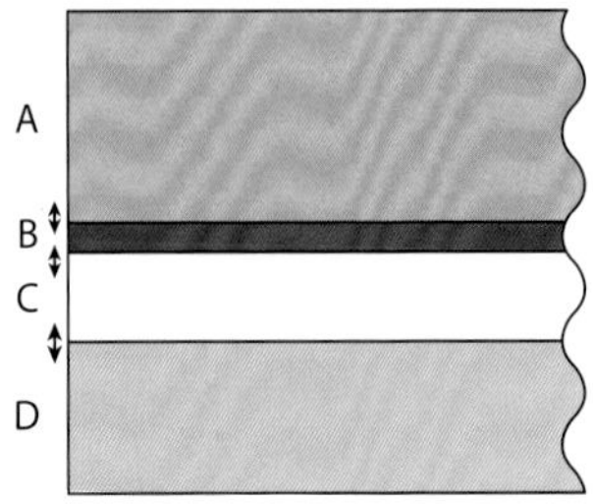

4. Cut twenty wedges, using the ruler technique described in Cutting Wedges (page 13).

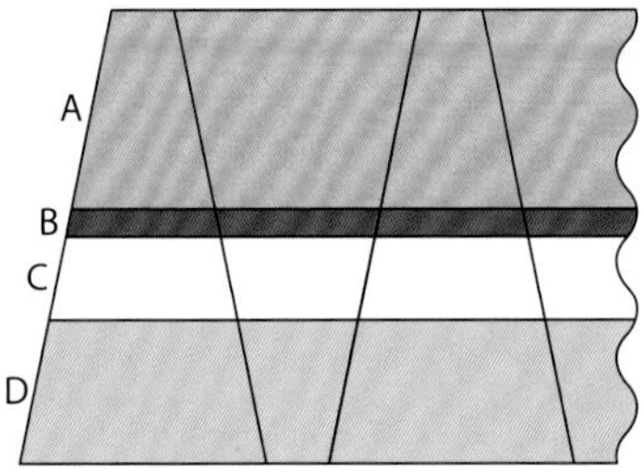

5. Separate the wedges into two sets by colorway.

6. Finish the edges as desired (see Edge Variations, page 17).

Note: *If a straight-edge plate is desired,* continue to Step 7. Before completing the center, choose either Method 1: Stay Stitching (page 19) or Method 2: Facing (page 20) to finish the edge.

7. Pair two wedges from each colorway RST. Position the wedge of the same colorway on top consistently for all ten pairs.

8. Sew all pairs together using the reverse stitching technique (page 21). Press the seams.

9. Join five pairs into half-circles and then half-circles to each other to create a plate. Complete the center (see The Dresden Center, page 27).

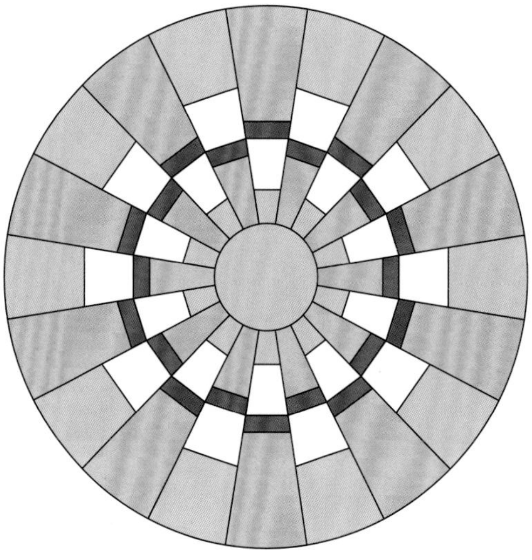

Traditional Bull's-Eye

Adding Single-Fabric Wedges

Symmetric four-fabric wedges in two colorways, alternating with single-fabric wedges

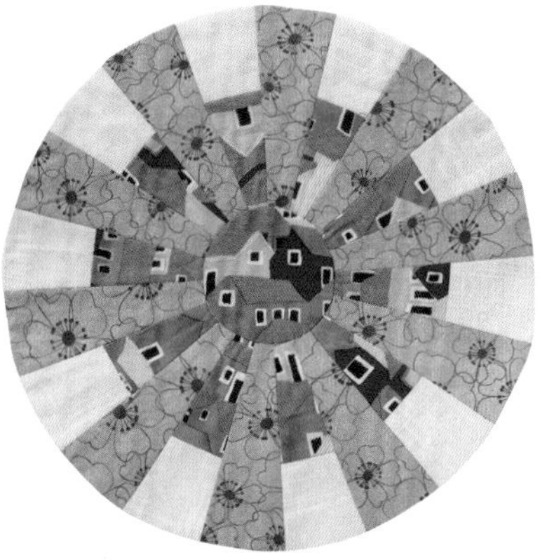

Symmetric two-fabric wedges, alternating with single-fabric wedges

Asymmetric four-fabric wedges, alternating with single-fabric wedges

Another simple, but dramatic piecing option can be universally applied to asymmetric- or symmetric-pieced wedges. It involves adding single-fabric wedges to the design. Mixing ten identical pieced wedges of the same colorway, for example, with ten single-fabric wedges in an additional fabric results in very striking blocks. The illusion of stacked circles peeking through a radiating grid is created. Yet another design emerges with this combination that is particularly dramatic looking when the single-fabric wedges are cut from one of the existing fabrics used in the strip set. This can be the perfect way to use a motif or directional fabric in pieced wedges. It's all about color, print, value, and repetition.

Construction

1. Make a pieced strip set with the desired number of fabrics (see Strip-Set Piecing, page 35).

2. Cut twenty wedges, using the ruler technique in Cutting Wedges (page 13).

3. Separate the wedges into two sets by colorway.

4. Cut a WOF strip from a single fabric the same width as the pieced strip set.

5. Cut twenty single-fabric wedges as in Step 2.

6. Add ten single-fabric wedges to each colorway set. Each colorway set now makes one complete Dresden plate.

7. Prepare the wedges with the desired edge finish (see Edge Variations, page 17).

Note: *If a straight-edge plate is desired,* continue to Steps 8–10. Before completing the center, choose either Method 1: Stay Stitching (page 19) or Method 2: Facing (page 20) to finish the edge.

8. Starting with one colorway set, pair a pieced wedge with a single-fabric wedge RST. Position the same wedge on top consistently for all ten pairs.

9. Sew the ten pairs together using the reverse stitching technique (page 21). Press the seams.

10. Join five pairs into half-circles and then half-circles to each other to create a plate. Complete the center (see The Dresden Center, page 27).

11. Follow Steps 7–10, using the other colorway set to make a second plate.

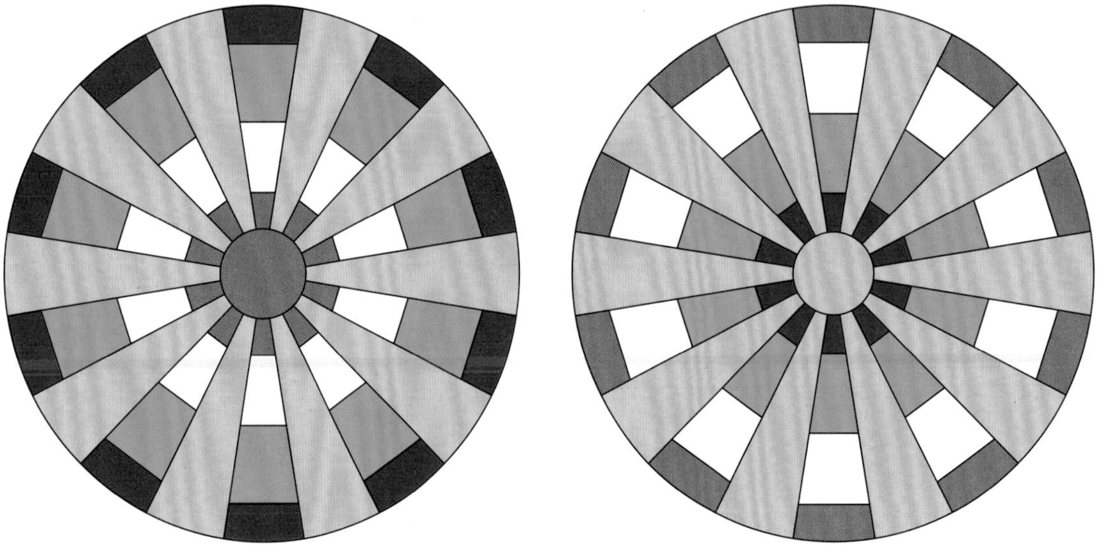

Two asymmetric blocks from the same pieced strip set;
pieced wedges of the same colorway, alternating with single-fabric wedges

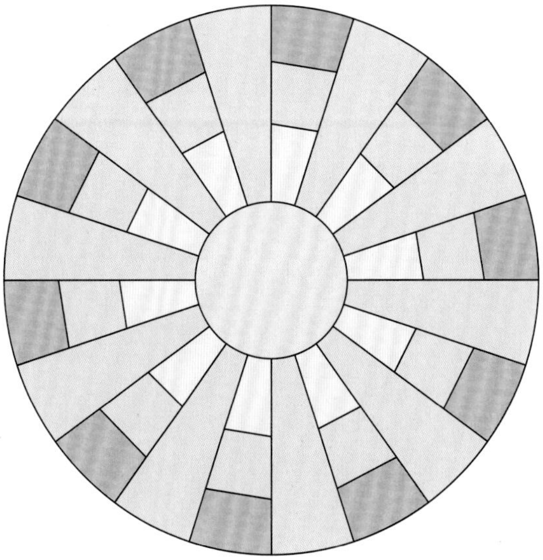

Symmetric three-fabric wedges,
alternating with single-fabric wedges

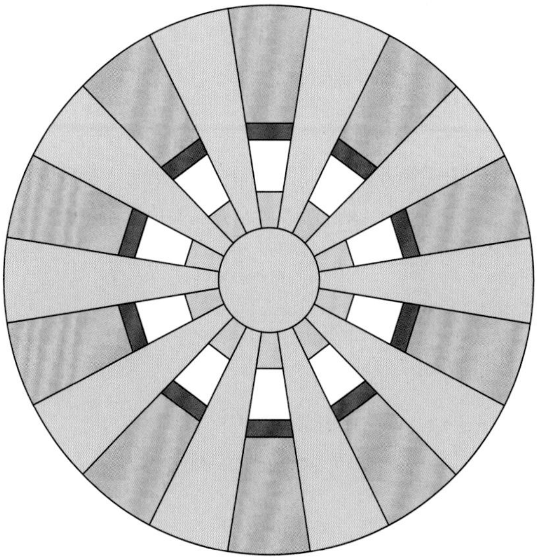

A Bull's-Eye wedge colorway
alternating with single-fabric wedges

Compass Rose

Four single-fabric wedges and two colorways
of asymmetric four-fabric wedges

Bull's-Eye / Compass Rose hybrid

One distinct plate stands out that uses the single-fabric wedge to define itself. That plate is the Compass Rose. Typically, a plate made with strip-pieced wedges, the Compass Rose has a single fabric positioned every fifth wedge, its four compass points. This block is immediately recognizable.

Construction

1. Cut a WOF strip from a single fabric (or from one of the fabrics used in the pieced wedges) the same width as the pieced strip set.

2. Cut four wedges, using the ruler technique described in Cutting Wedges (page 13).

3. Prepare the wedges with the desired edge finish (see Edge Variations, page 17).

Note: *If a straight-edge plate is desired*, continue to Steps 4–6. Choose either Method 1: Stay Stitching (page 19) or Method 2: Facing (page 20) to finish the edge. Then complete Step 7.

4. Select a wedge from each colorway and pair RST. Make eight pairs—all of which have the wedge of the same colorway on top.

5. Sew pairs together using the reverse stitching technique (page 21). Press the seams.

6. Lay out two pairs followed by one single-fabric wedge. Join to make a quarter-plate. Make three more identical quarter-plates. Join all four quarter-plates to make a Compass Rose.

7. Complete the center (see The Dresden Center, page 27).

Bull's-Eye / Compass Rose hybrid

tip Centers can be made from the outer edge fabric or any fabric of your choice.

Single-Wedge Piecing

This next group of pieced wedge Dresden blocks requires each wedge to be pieced individually—unlike employing strip sets that produce multiple wedges. These individually pieced wedges can involve a mixture of techniques, but in the end, each wedge must be created one by one. Another feature of this Dresden group is that the piecing has been liberated from the standard horizontal seam that spans the width of the wedge. The wedge now has vertical and slanted seams too.

Split-Wedge Dresden

The Split-Wedge is a dynamic design featuring two *high-contrast* fabrics pieced lengthwise within each wedge. It can be used to form the centerpiece of a layout because it is so dramatic. Careful planning is important to determine the necessary yardage; careful layout and cutting are important to maintain the design's consistent pattern; and, of course, careful pressing is important with twice the usual number of seams. You can do it!

Although the Split-Wedge plate thinks of itself as a pieced strip-set block, in the final analysis, its Dresden wedges are formed one at a time. To start off, strip sets are sewn; then they're cut into segments; and lastly, each segment must be fashioned into a wedge.

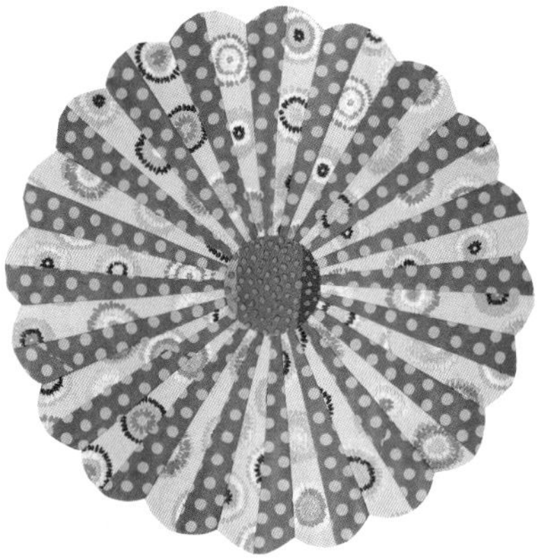

CUTTING SPLIT-WEDGES

Wedge size	Fabrics A and B		
	Strip width	Strip sets	Yardage
4″	1¾″	2	⅛
5″	1¾″	3	¼
6″	1¾″	4	¼
7″	2″	4	¼
8″	2″	4	¼
9″	2¼″	5	⅓

Construction

1. Decide the wedge size you want. Cut WOF strips from each fabric according to the Cutting Split-Wedges chart (at left).

2. Sew Fabric strips A and B lengthwise together. Press the seams open. Complete the number of strip sets as directed in the chart.

3. Subcut the pieced strip sets into twenty segments to the desired wedge size.

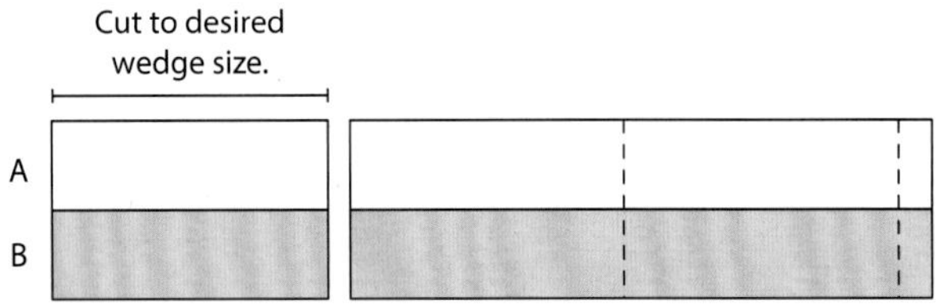

4. Cut the wedges from the segments taking care to keep the fabric orientation identical each time.

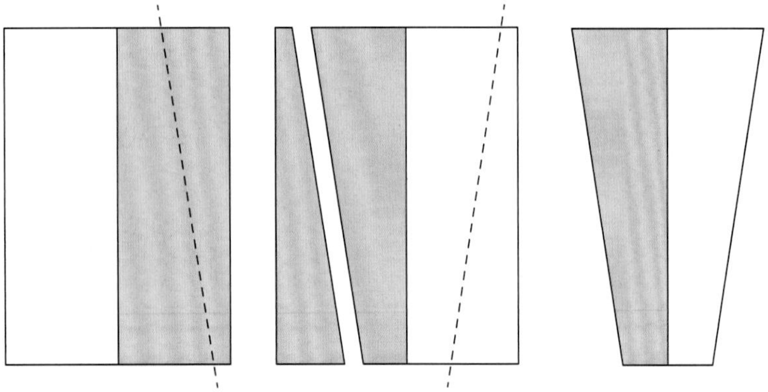

tip A rotating cutting mat is very helpful when cutting the individual wedges.

---

5. Finish the edges as desired (see Edge Variations, page 17).

Note: *If a straight-edge plate is desired*, continue to Steps 6 and 7. Before completing the center, choose either Method 1: Stay Stitching (page 19) or Method 2: Facing (page 20) to finish the edge.

6. Pair two wedges RST. Sew pairs together using the reverse stitching technique (page 21). Press the seams.

7. Join five pairs into half-circles and then half-circles to each other to create a plate. Complete the center (see, The Dresden Center, page 27).

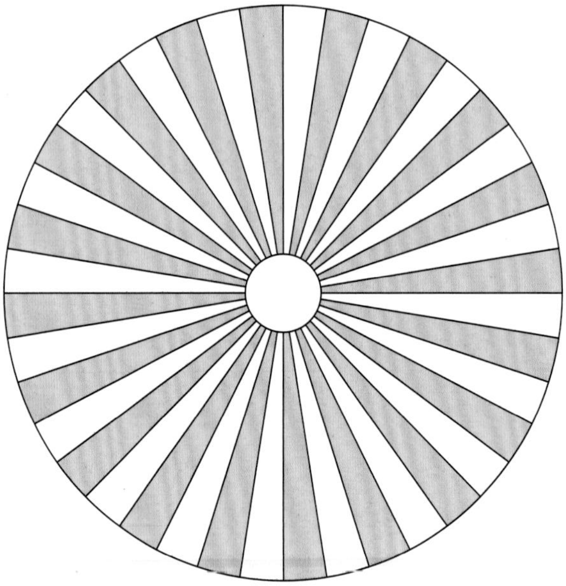

Split-Wedge plate

tip Use a pressing bar (page 72) and press the seams open to prevent seam bulk.

Sawtooth Dresden

Sawtooth Dresdens have a spinning, circular appearance. They are made with two *contrasting* fabrics. The finished plate looks very different depending on which fabric is placed on the inside of the block.

To create this block, the pieced wedge is formed using two rectangles sewn together on a 45° angle. Like the Split-Wedge Dresden, the Sawtooth wedges are then trimmed from each unit. Wedge size varies 5″–9″, and all edge finishes are suitable.

CUTTING SAWTOOTH WEDGE RECTANGLES

Wedge size	Fabrics A and B		
	Strips	Strip size	Subcut into 20 rectangles
5″	2	2⅜″	3⅝″
6″	3	2¾″	4⅜″
7″	3	3″	5″
8″	4	3⅜″	5¾″
9″	4	3¾″	6⅜″

Construction

1. Select two contrasting fabrics and determine the desired wedge size. (See the Plate Sizes and Traditional Backgrounds chart, page 14.) Refer to the Cutting Sawtooth Wedge Rectangles chart (page 49) to cut 20 *rectangles* from each fabric based on the desired wedge size.

2. Place two different fabric rectangles RST at a 90° angle to each other so their top and right edges align. Be consistent in placing the same fabric on top. Draw a diagonal line as shown.

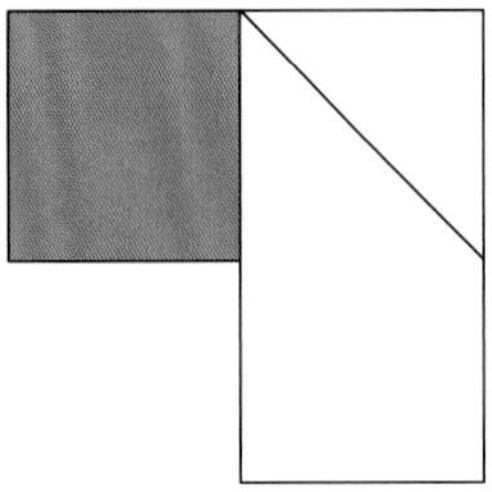

3. Sew on the drawn line. Press toward the darker color.

4. Trim away the excess fabric, leaving a ¼″ seam allowance.

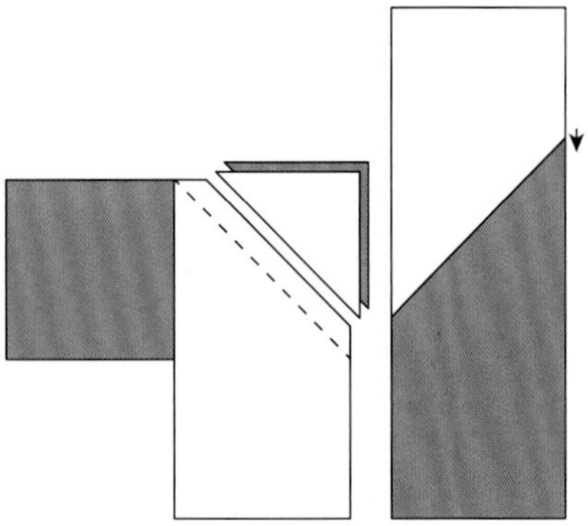

5. Decide which fabric you want to form the outer edge of the block and position the strip so the widest end of the Dresden ruler is always positioned on this fabric. Line up the wide end of the ruler with the narrow side of the wedge unit. Cut each wedge identically.

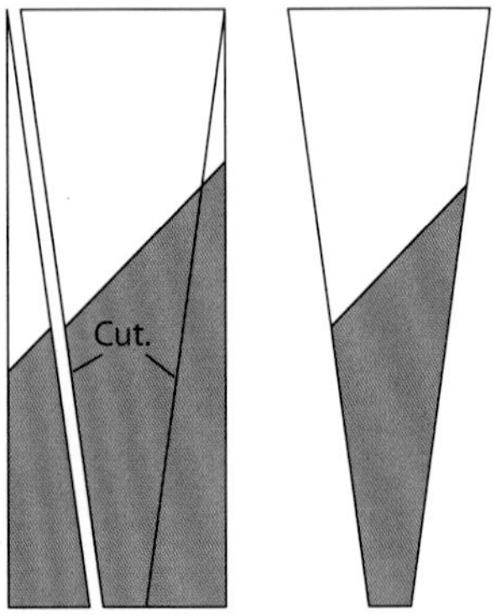

tip A rotating cutting mat is very helpful when making individual wedges.

6. Finish the block, following Split-Wedge Dresden, Construction, Steps 3–6 (page 48).

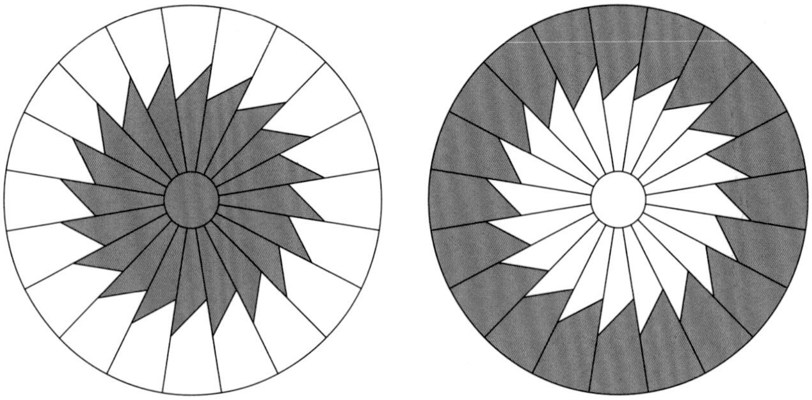

Flying Geese Dresden

The Flying Geese Dresden belongs squarely in the group of plates whose wedges are individually pieced. Based loosely on the Dresden Sawtooth, it has a dramatic circular effect when done in two high-contrast fabrics so that the Geese circle clockwise. Foundation piecing is the key to keeping the points sharp and the Geese circling. This block can be made using three different size wedges: 8″, 8½″, or 9″. Read through all the instructions and refer to the photos before starting the block.

tip Solids or fabrics that read as solids work well for the Geese.

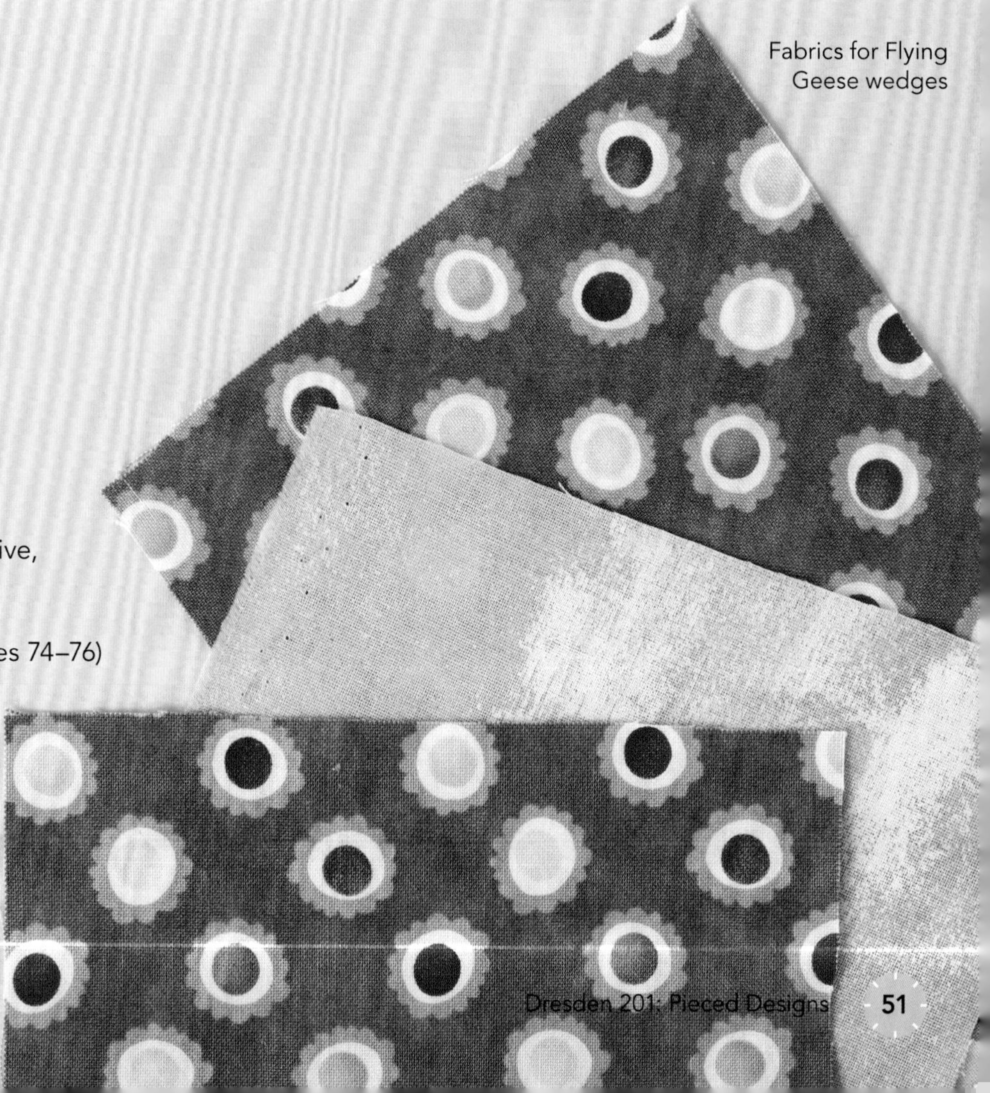

Fabrics for Flying Geese wedges

MATERIALS

Flying Geese

For 8½″ and 9″ wedges:

- Fabric A (background): ⅞ yard
- Fabric B (Flying Geese): ¼ yard

For 8″ wedges:

- Fabric A (background): ⅝ yard
- Fabric B (Flying Geese): ¼ yard

Other supplies

- Foundation papers or inexpensive, thin typing paper
- Wedge template patterns (pages 74–76) in the desired wedge size
- Glue stick

CUTTING

8″ wedges

Fabric A

- Cut 3 WOF strips 3″ wide. Subcut into 20 rectangles 3″ × 5″ for section 1.
- Cut 2 WOF strips 5½″ wide. Subcut into 20 rectangles 5½″ × 4″ for section 3.

Fabric B

- Cut 2 WOF strips 3″ wide. Subcut into 20 rectangles 3″ × 3½″ for section 2.

8½″ wedges

Fabric A

- Cut 3 WOF strips 3″ wide. Subcut into 20 rectangles 3″ × 5″ for section 1.
- Cut 3 WOF strips 6″ wide. Subcut into 20 rectangles 6″ × 4½″ for section 3.

Fabric B

- Cut 2 WOF strips 3″ wide. Subcut into 20 rectangles 3″ × 3½″ for section 2.

9″ wedges

Fabric A

- Cut 2 WOF strips 5″ wide. Subcut into 20 rectangles 5″ × 3½″ for section 1.
- Cut 3 WOF strips 6″ wide. Subcut into 20 rectangles 6″ × 4½″ for section 3.

Fabric B

- Cut 2 WOF strips 3½″ wide. Subcut into 20 rectangles 3½″ × 4″ for section 2.

Construction

1. Shorten the stitch length on your sewing machine to 2.0.

2. Trace or photocopy the desired size wedge template pattern (pages 74–76) onto foundation papers enough times to make twenty wedges. Cut out beyond the solid line of each wedge.

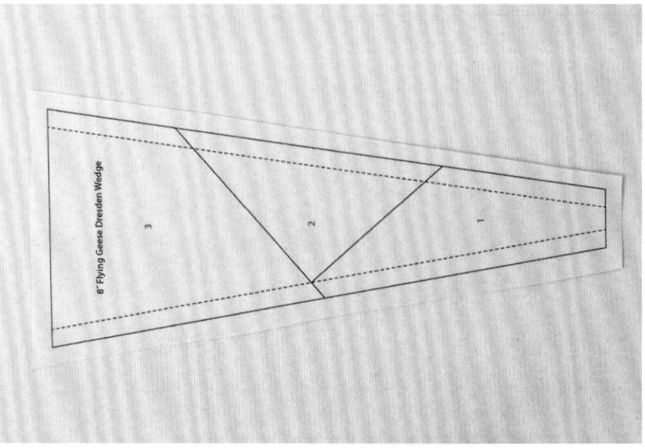

3. Work on one wedge at a time. The marked side of the template is the sewing side; the *numbers* are the piecing order; and the solid *lines* between spaces are stitching lines. Fabric is placed on the back of the sewing side.

4. Lay the printed side of the foundation pattern facedown. Place Fabric A over section 1, right side up. The edges of the fabric rectangle should extend at least ¼″ beyond the seamlines. Use a glue stick or pin to hold the fabric piece in place. Holding the entire piece up to the light helps with placement.

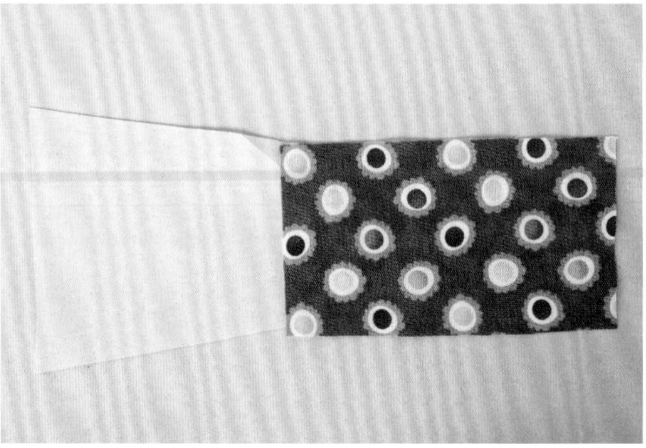

Fabric rectangle A covering section 1 of foundation paper

5. Place Fabric B onto Fabric A, RST, at the stitching line between sections 1 and 2. Both fabrics should extend at least ¼″ into space 2. Make sure it covers the Geese section 2 when it's flipped. Pin.

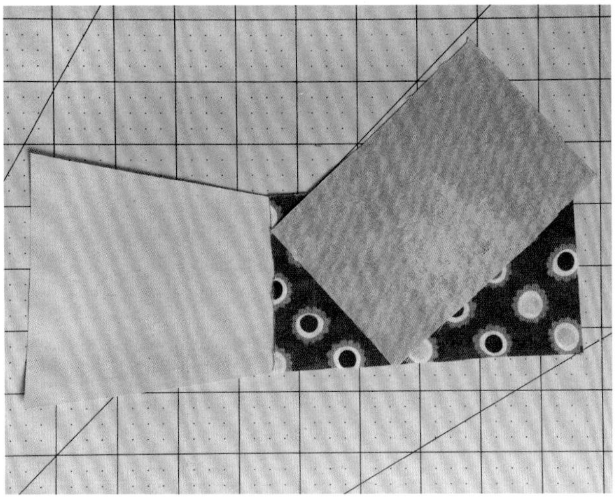

Fabrics A and B, RST, covering section 1

6. With the printed side of the foundation paper facing you, stitch on the sewing line between sections 1 and 2, beginning and ending a few stitches past the dashed outer seamline.

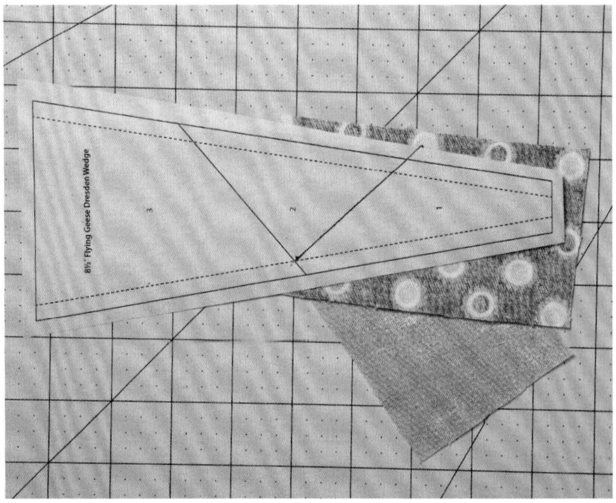

Flip the foundation to stitch on line between sections 1 and 2.

7. Open Fabric B out and check to see that it completely covers section 2 and extends at least ¼″ beyond the seamlines of section 2. Fold the paper back along the stitched line to trim the seam allowance to ¼″. Do not cut the paper. Press well with a dry iron.

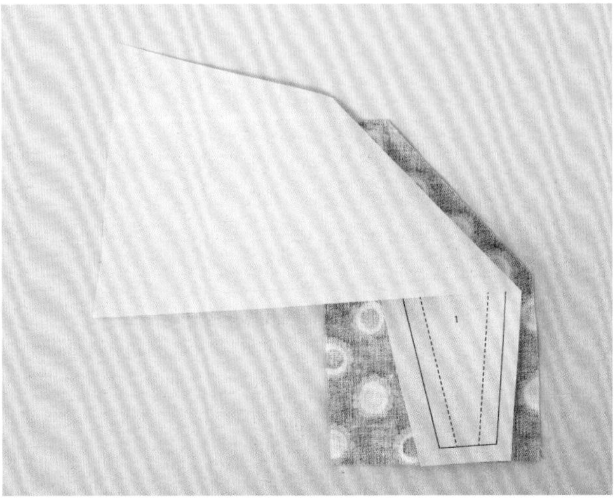

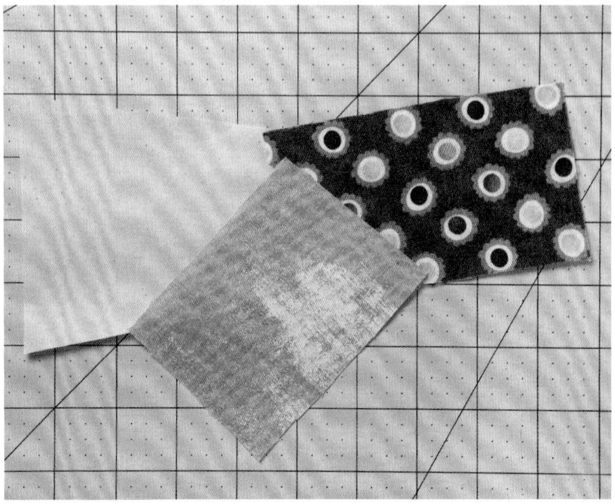

Fabrics A and B opened and pressed

8. Follow the same process to add Fabric C to section 3.

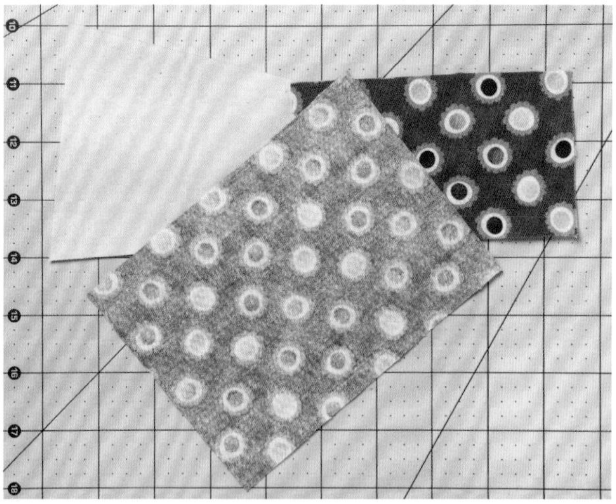

Placing Fabric C

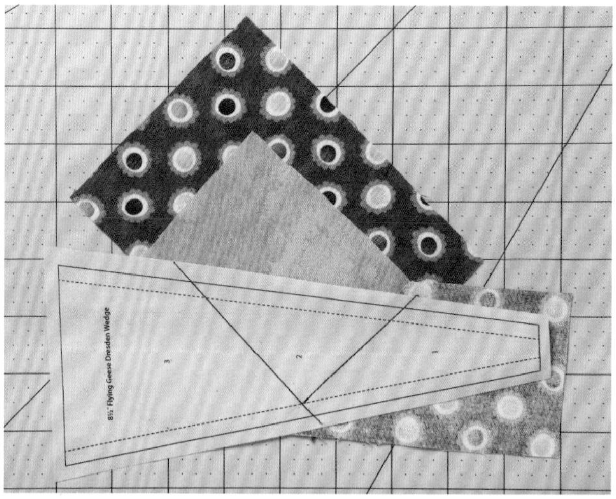

Flip the foundation; sew on seamline between 2 and 3

9. Press the seams with a dry iron.

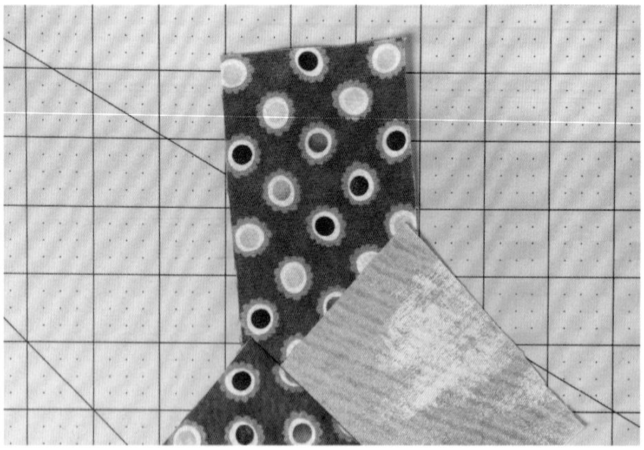

Fabric-covered wedge

10. Trim the entire wedge on the outer solid line.

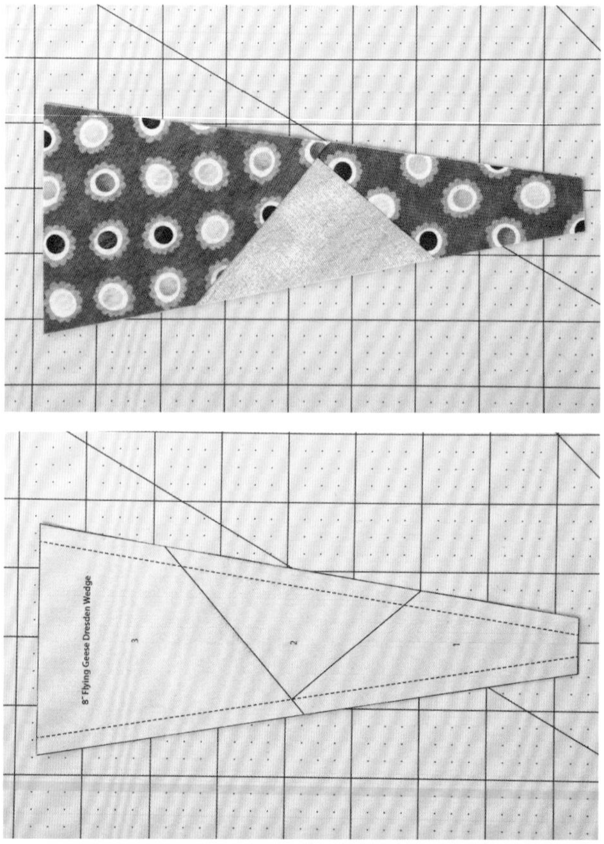

Trimmed wedge, front and back

11. Repeat Steps 3–10 for a total of twenty wedges.

12. Prepare the wedges with the desired edge finish (see Edge Variations, page 17).

Note: *If a straight-edge plate is desired,* continue to Steps 13–16. After removing foundation papers, choose either Method 1: Stay Stitching (page 19) or Method 2: Facing (page 20) to finish the outer edge.

13. Pair two wedges RST. Repeat for a total of ten pairs.

14. Sew the ten pairs together using the reverse stitching technique (page 21). Before pressing the seams, remove the foundation paper in the seam allowance. Use a pressing bar for crisp, flat seams.

15. Join five pairs into half-circles and then half-circles to each other to create a plate.

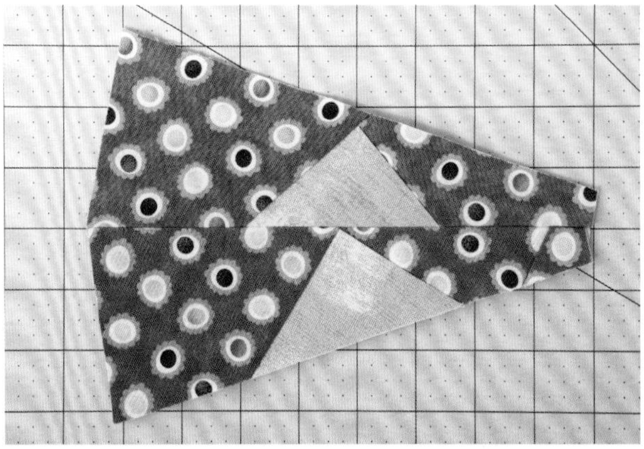

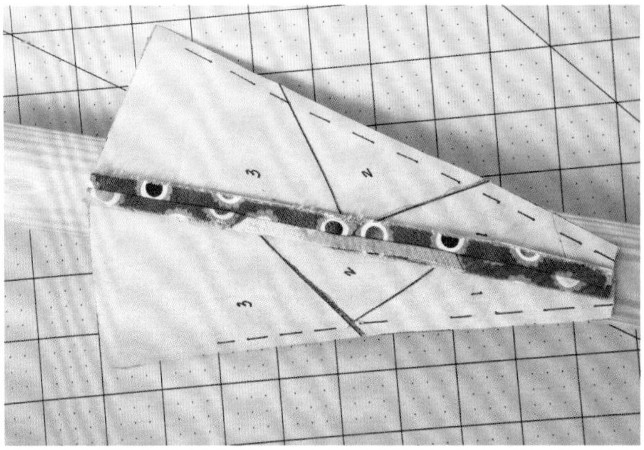

Two wedges stitched and pressed open

16. Remove foundation papers carefully. Stabilize the opening and add the center (see The Dresden Center, page 27).

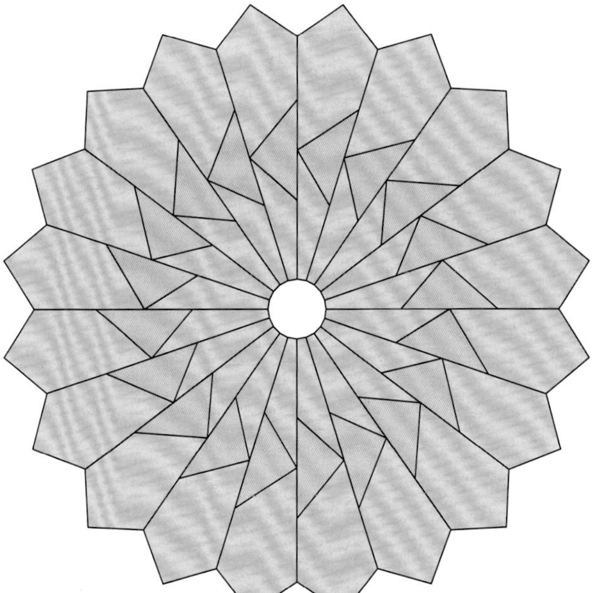

Completed Flying Geese Dresden

THERE'S MORE *to be done*

The Dresden design is not just for single round plates. The wedge shape that is the basis of the plate can be manipulated in other ways to create additional designs. Some design options include stacking, layering, or overlapping plates to use in modern settings; joining five or ten wedges for quarter- or half-circle blocks; or even sewing wedges together flipping their orientation to create a column design which can be used in borders, quilts, or table runners.

Layered Blocks

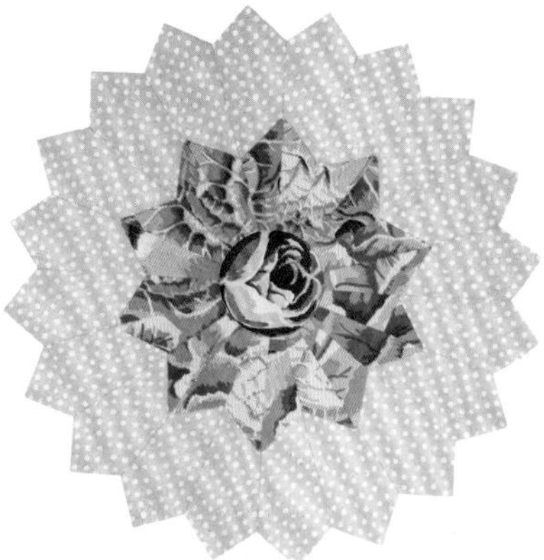  

Layering plates can increase your design options tenfold. I first figured this out when I had a 22″ yellow-and-orange plate made from one fabric. It had to be covered! It screamed and stood out. Since that fortunate mistake I have gone on to layer many plates some even with three layers! It creates depth and interest and is a fun way to use many different fabrics.

Any edge design can be layered with another, but the most common are: straight edges topped by points or curved edges; three-sided edges topped by straight, curved, or pointed edges; or even straight edges on top of straight edges.

Construction

1. First complete the plates, following Cutting Wedges (page 13) and Straight-Edge Plate, Construction (page 18).

2. Stabilize the center openings, but do not add the centers yet.

3. Line up a smaller plate on top of a larger plate by matching the seamlines all the way around.

4. Pin carefully and appliqué the small plate to the larger one.

5. Add a center after layering is complete.

tip Alternately, with a pointed-edge plate, the points can line up to the seamlines of the larger plate. Pin the layers carefully in many places. Secure the top plate in place with a hand whipstitch, invisible machine appliqué, or decorative stitch.

Partial Blocks

The wedge design can be used for quarter- or half-circle designs.

Piece five wedges together and appliqué them to a background block to create a fan, which can be used in the corner of a quilt or in blocks throughout a quilt.

Piece ten wedges together and appliqué them to a background to create a half-circle, which can be used on the edges of quilts to bring the design elements to the edge and beyond.

Borders or Straight Piecing

Wedges can be sewn together in the same orientation as they were cut to create a straight line. This can be used for a border, a row in a quilt, a table runner, or an entire quilt. Lower the wedge ruler at the bottom of the fabric's edge to the 1″ or 2″ line. This results in a different shape wedge that still sews together in a straight line.

Complete plate border

Candy Stripes Grown Up 49″ × 49″, made and quilted by Candyce Copp Grisham

Extending the Size of the Wedge

If you want a 10″ or 22″ wedge, first cut a WOF strip the desired size. Place a longer straight ruler on the side of the Dresden ruler to extend the length. Remove the Dresden ruler and make the first cut. Replace the Dresden ruler and repeat for the next side. A rotating rotary mat is very helpful. The edge finishes are just the same as for smaller wedges.

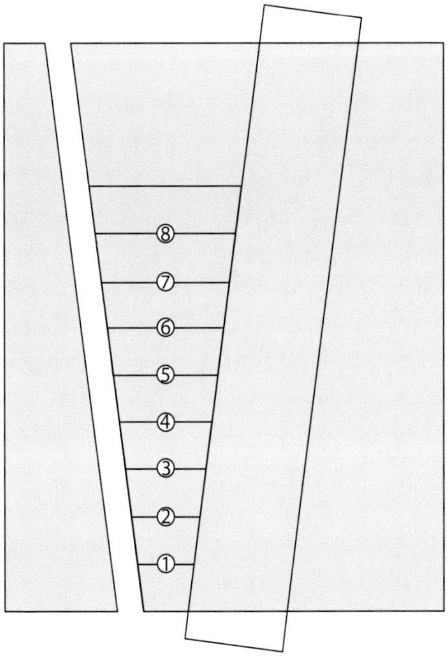

Extending the size of the wedge

Repurposed Fabrics

Have you ever come across a bundle of fabrics that never made it into a finished product or a pieced top that was never quilted? These can be repurposed into wedges then into blocks. I found a bag of vintage 30's fabrics cut out for a double wedding ring quilt but never sewn together. These were easy to cut into 3″ wedges and reassembled into blocks for a wonderful collection of vintage Dresdens.

30's fabrics

Fun Ideas for Using Dresden Blocks

Now that you have started making blocks you might be wondering about how you can use them. Here are a few ideas.

- Make a quilt or wallhanging. Look at the quilts in the Gallery (page 62) for inspiration. The blocks can be laid out in a very random or in a more controlled manner. They can be mixed in size or color or be the same throughout.
- Blocks can be appliquéd to background squares and sewn into a traditional quilt.
- Blocks can be laid out in a pattern that resembles a garden or starry sky. Think about fireworks!
- Make a raffle or opportunity quilt. An entire group of quilters can each make one or two plates and then combine them into one quilt. This is a great way to support your guild or organization. Encourage participation and don't worry about everyone's seam allowance matching. Backgrounds can be divided into smaller units to make the appliqué process faster.
- Use the blocks as a block-of-the-month program. Start with the basics, like cutting the wedges and then move onto different edge treatments and Dresden 201 blocks. Students can create their own blocks and then make a final project.
- Use the block ideas as a guild challenge. It could be based simply on the Dresden block or limited by color, edge treatment, or number of blocks. It could even be a distortion or change of the basic block.
- Have a block exchange. A group could participate in making several of each block and then exchange them with friends or with an online group. You end up with more blocks this way and more variety too.
- Round-robins are fun. A group could start with a large Dresden as a center block and pass it to other members in the group who would layer additional Dresdens or complete border treatments.

Thank you for going on the Dresden journey with me. I hope you have a lot of fun.

Candy

GALLERY

SERVICE FOR 12 78½″ × 95″, made for the Rambling River Art Quilters Challenge by Tracy Back, Joan Ferguson, Candyce Copp Grisham, Klonda Holt, Judy Humphrey, Jane Kennedy, Sharon Neur, Cheri Raybourn, Terry Rhodes, Wendy Carter Richards, Nancy Sinise, and Cathy Wight; quilted by Candyce Copp Grisham

Pieced background. *Dresdens:* Uses 45 blocks total, straight, round, pointed, split, Cogwheel, layered, mixed edges. *Center treatments:* Hexagons, offset circles, fussy-cut florals, and so on. Individuals made two or three blocks each and then appliquéd blocks to background.

CANDY AND FIREWORKS 32″ × 40″, made by Klonda Holt

Beautiful hand dyed background. *Dresdens:* Uses 12 plates 3½″–6″, straight, pointed, layers, mixed edges, round, Split-Wedges, irregular binding that includes overhanging plate.

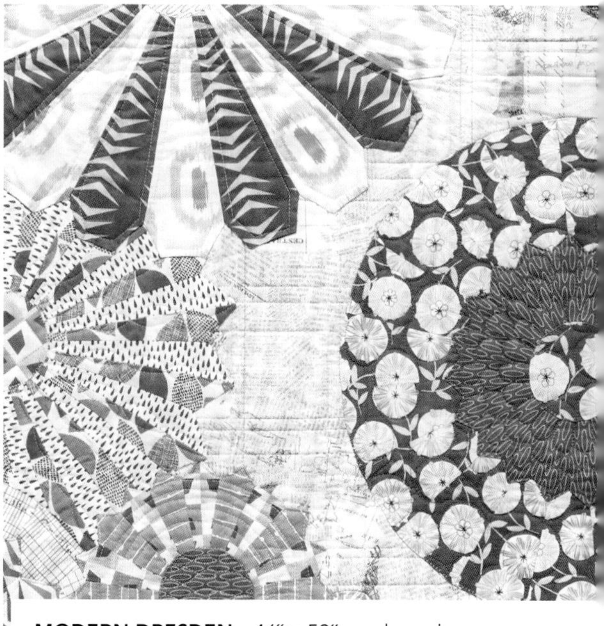

MODERN DRESDEN 46″ × 52″, made and quilted by Candyce Copp Grisham

Pieced background with 11 plates. *Dresdens:* Straight, pointed, round, split, three-sided, and layered. Done in a more monochromatic color palate to reflect modern fabrics.

DRESDEN SPRING TIME 36″ × 39″, made and quilted by Candyce Copp Grisham

Pieced background. *Dresdens:* Uses 7 plates with straight, pointed, split, round, and layered wedges, corner fans, 14 small circles appliquéd by machine in blanket stitch.

DRESDENS AND FANS 42″ × 54″, made by Judy Brinker

Includes plates made with 9° wedge by Marilyn Doheny. *Dresdens:* Multiple plates; pointed, round, layered, split, circles, wonderful examples of overlapping and half-circles.

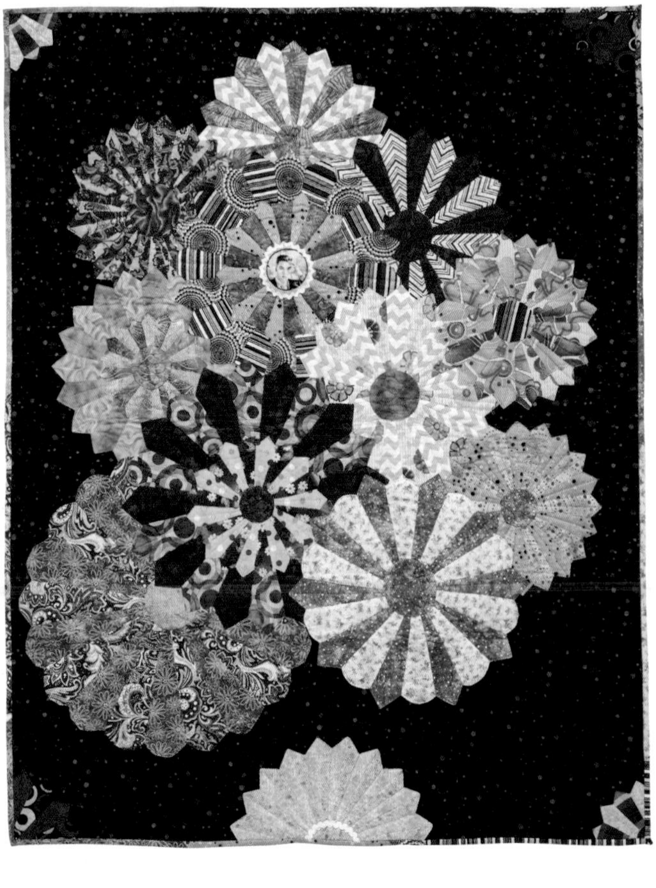

Detail of Elvis medallion in *Modern Dresden Plates*

MODERN DRESDEN PLATES 41″ × 52″, made by Barbara Harrell

Dresdens: Uses 14 plates with round, mixed edges, pointed, plus half- and quarter-circles. Barb added Elvis and other fun trims to the centers of the blocks.

DANCING DRESDENS 44″ × 57″, made by Candyce Copp Grisham

Uses 3 Dresden plates and pieced border; piped border. This design is a great way to show off a line of fabrics and to show off your quilting in the negative background space.

DRESDEN SPLASH 62″ × 62″, made by Michele Weiland

Traditional pieced background with plates symmetrically placed. *Dresdens:* Uses 17 plates, all pointed, 11 layered.

DRESDEN DELIGHT 31½″ × 62″,
made by Catherine Fueglin

Beautiful rich batik plates on an ombré batik background. Cathy invented a new block by partially finishing the sides of some wedges.

STEAMPUNK COGWHEEL
86″ × 100″, made by Candyce Copp Grisham, quilted by Jane Coons

Original design by author; Cogwheels on 15″ background blocks set on point; 18 blocks; pieced borders. The challenge was to make a block quilt using one of the Dresden variations.

PACHYDERM PARTY 49″ × 66½″, made by Becky Whiteside

One background fabric. *Dresdens:* Single, round, pointed, three-sided; pieced plates with lots of trim, original centers, and elephants!

PATRIOTIC HONOR FLIGHT QUILT 34″ × 34″, made by Judy Humphrey

Judy used three-layered, pointed plates as the center motif on one of her Honor Flight quilts given to veterans as they fly to Washington, DC.

SERENDIPITY 24″ × 46″, made and quilted by Candyce Copp Grisham

Two Serendipity blocks pieced round-robin style for a small wallhanging.

DANCING DRESDEN 50″ × 59″, made by Adele Niblack

Uses 11 blocks on an all-black background. *Dresdens:* One corner block, reverse appliquéd center, and three-dimensional edges.

DRESDEN BLOOM 52″ × 46″, made by Candyce Copp Grisham

An enlarged single Dresden block with 20″ wedges that stands alone.

MIDNIGHT IN THE GARDEN WITH FRIENDS 72″ × 72″, made by Candyce Copp Grisham

Examples of pieced wedges, all using batiks on a solid black background. *Dresdens:* Uses 43 different blocks with straight, pointed, and curved edges.

EVERYTHING *you need to know*

Troubleshooting

Problem	Solutions
Not enough fabric for required wedges.	Piece the fabric large enough to cut out the wedges.
	Find a similar fabric and add several wedges to even out the arrangement.
	Use 3 colors and use the chosen fabric for 5 wedges, adding in other colors.
Finished plate does not lie flat. It has a volcano or hat appearance.	Count the number of wedges. Often one or two extra may have been added.
	Take in the seams with a very narrow stitch until it lies flat. You can often see which is the offending seam.
	Make sure you are cutting accurately and sewing a full ¼″ seam.
Block stands out in a way that is not appealing.	Layer another block on top.
	Think about changing the center.
	Make another block in its place.
Points aren't pointed enough.	Reduce the bulk in the seam allowance at the fold area. Carefully use a point turner to make a sharp point.
Curves are not smooth.	Sew with a shorter stitch length and stitch continuously around the curve. No stops and turns.
	Trim the seam allowance to ⅛″.
	Gently use the smooth edge of a point turner to smooth out the curve and press.
When making the 3-sided edge, the ruler is hard to place in the correct place.	Make a template of the cutout corner and use it each time to line up the ruler.
	Put tape on the ruler to help position it.
Not sure how many blocks to make.	Make a lot of blocks in different sizes, color combinations, and edges. You won't use them all, but you can any save leftovers for another project.

Glossary of Terms

Block A completed Dresden plate, generally with twenty wedges.

Chain piecing The process of sewing a continuous series of units together without breaking the thread between. Chain piecing conserves thread and time since one seam is sewn right after another.

Colorway For our purposes, it refers to two of the same item but in colors or fabrics that are in reversed order.

Dresden 201 Dresden blocks that have more piecing, designs, or layers than simple Dresdens and can have any edge finish.

Edge The outside edge of the Dresden plates. Edges can be straight, pointed, curved, and three-sided. All are completed by machine.

Fat quarter (FQ) A standard cut of fabric usually 18″ × 22″.

Fussy cut Cutting a particular area of fabric to highlight a certain motif. It is often used to repeat a pattern through a block.

Needle-turn appliqué The technique of turning under the raw edge of fabric and using a hand sewing needle to take small stitches to secure it to background fabric.

Nonwoven, nonfusible interfacing Such as Pellon 906F, popular as a facing and a stabilizer.

Plate I use interchangeably with *block* and, for our purposes, refers to a Dresden circle made of twenty wedges cut at an 18° angle.

Reverse stitching This technique is used to begin a seam ¼″ down from an edge, stitching in reverse to that edge and then forward for the length of the seam (see Note: Reverse Stitching Technique, page 21).

Right sides together (RST) The way two pieces of fabric are positioned with their right sides facing when cutting or sewing.

Serendipity block A ten-pointed Dresden block that employs two wedges to create a large point.

Wedges Individual units cut with an acrylic ruler that make up a Dresden plate.

Wedge size The height or length of a wedge. Most Dresden rulers provide wedge sizes marked in ¼″ increments.

Whipstitch A small (⅛″- to ¼″-long), hand-sewn stitch taken on the edge of folded fabric to secure the piece to underlying fabric.

Width of fabric (WOF) The measurement of fabric from selvage to selvage, generally 40″–44″.

Clipping Tool for Chain Piecing

Using a clipping tool helps save wear and tear on your hands while you separate chain-pieced units from each other.

Two homemade clipping tools that you can make yourself

For a quick chain piecing tool: Place a seam ripper, cutting blade up, in the hole in the center of a spool of thread. Be sure to find a spool that holds the seam ripper snugly. Use this tool at your side to cut the threads of your chain-pieced units.

To make a more substantial piecing tool: Use a 2½″ hole saw with a ¼″ arbor* to cut a hole in a scrap of pinewood, minimum ¾″ thick; retrieve the plug as a base for your thread cutter. The center hole will hold a *small* seam ripper, which will stand securely to allow easy thread clipping.

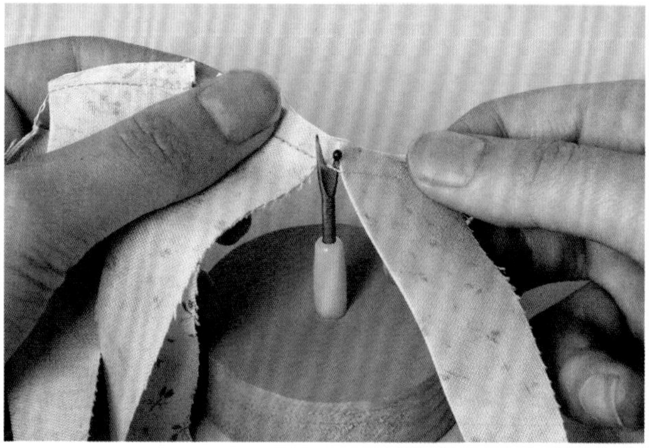

** An arbor is the standard drill bit that sits in the center of the hole saw and helps start the cut. It is used to stabilize the hole saw and makes the center hole for your seam ripper as the saw cuts the plug.*

Pressing Bar

All wedge seams should be pressed open on a hard, narrow surface. This is the best way to make a crisp seam and avoid pressing other seams incorrectly. You can purchase a pressing bar (see Resources, page 78) or make your own. The simplest way to create a pressing bar is with supplies easily obtainable at your local hardware store.

Buy an 8-foot section of pine wall-mounted hand railing. Have it cut or cut it yourself into 14″ sections. The flat portion will sit well on an ironing surface and the seam can easily be pressed open. Share the extra lengths with your friends or guild members.

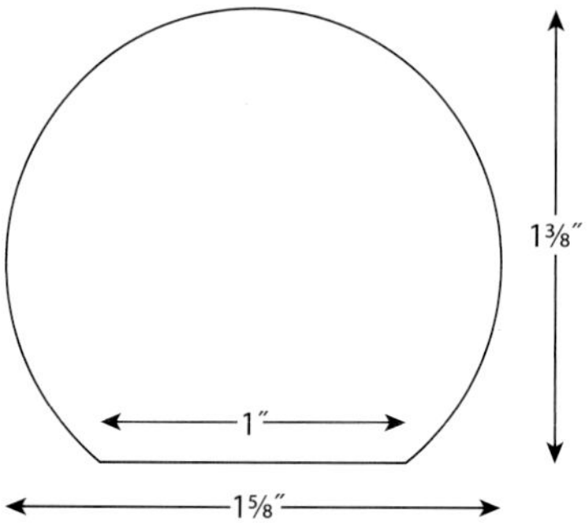

Cross section of pine wall-mounted handrail

Center Placement Tool

1. Cut out a 12″ square of freezer paper.

2. Fold it in half and half again so there are 4 equal quadrants. Draw on the fold lines to mark the quarters.

3. Use a template in the desired size to trace a circle in the center of the square, using the fold lines for registration.

4. Cut out the traced circle.

5. Center the prepared placement tool over the Dresden plate, aligning its marked fold lines to 4 of the plate's seamlines.

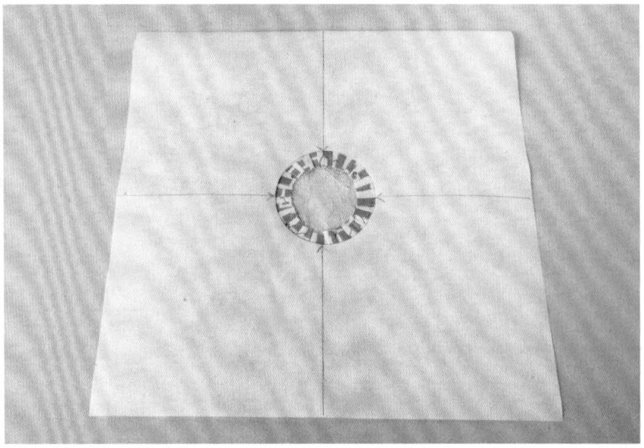

Centering placement tool

6. Place the finished fabric center in the opening and pin or fuse it in place.

7. Remove the freezer paper placement tool.

8. Stitch the center in place, using your preferred method.

Centering Tool for Points

There are various metal triangles used for pressing Dresden points that you can purchase, but you can make your own for a fraction of the cost.

1. Use stiff card stock to cut out an index card–size rectangle, about 4″ × 6″.

2. Place the 45° line of a ruler along the card's edge and slide the ruler's edge to a corner. Draw a 45° line with a permanent marker from the corner, about 3″ long.

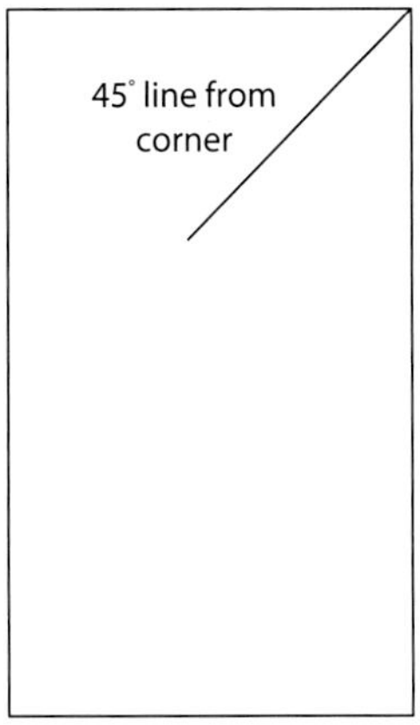

3. For perfect points, work from the wrong side of the wedge. Insert the card's marked corner into the wedge's point.

4. Line up the seam with the drawn line and press with a hot, dry iron.

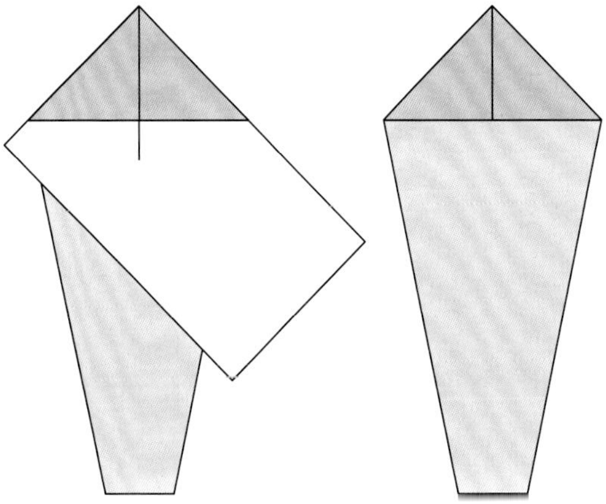

TEMPLATE PATTERNS

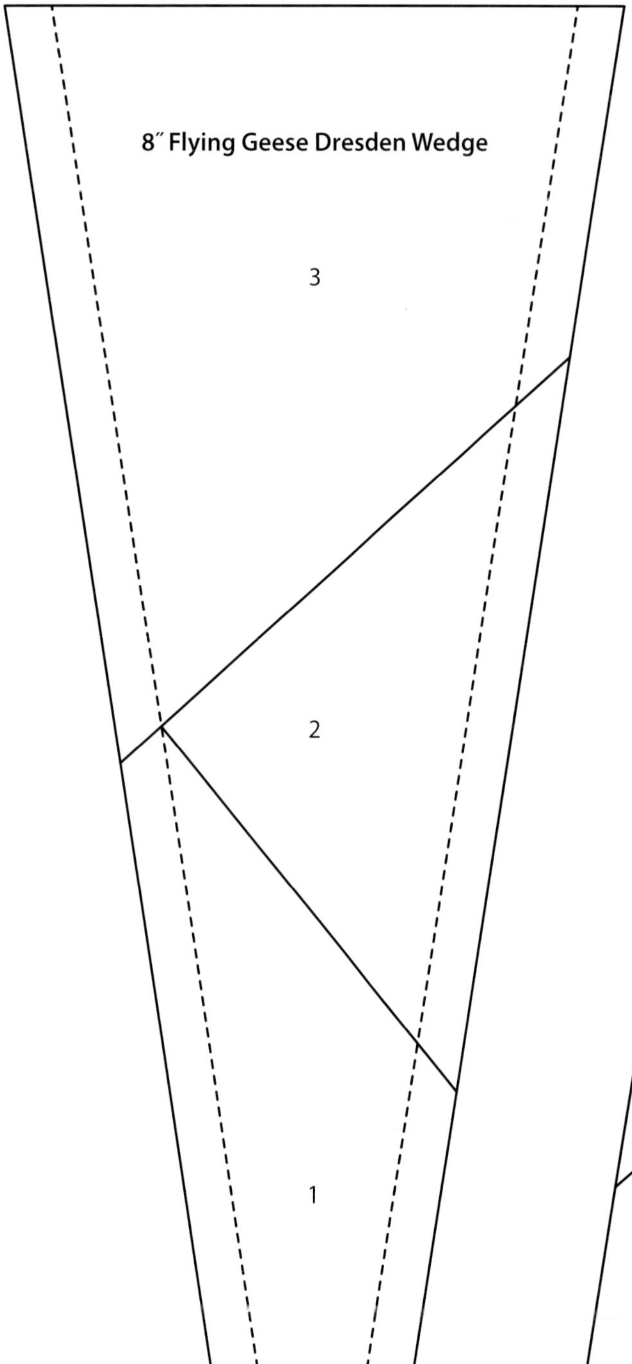

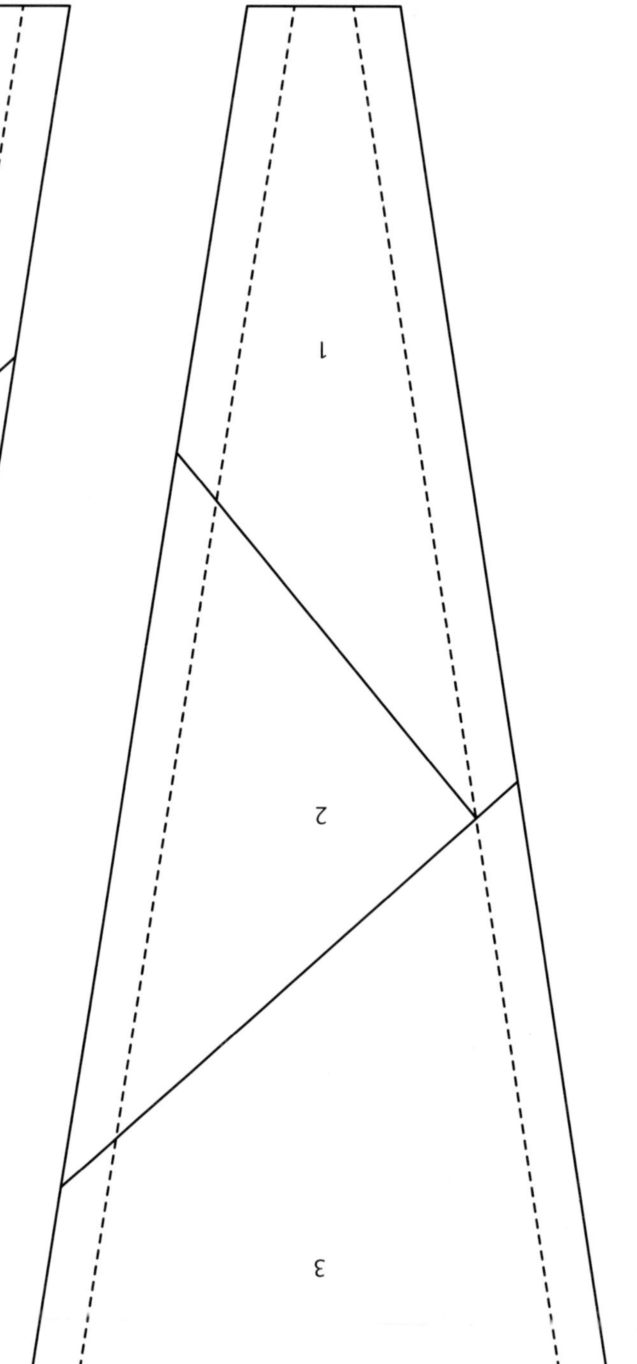

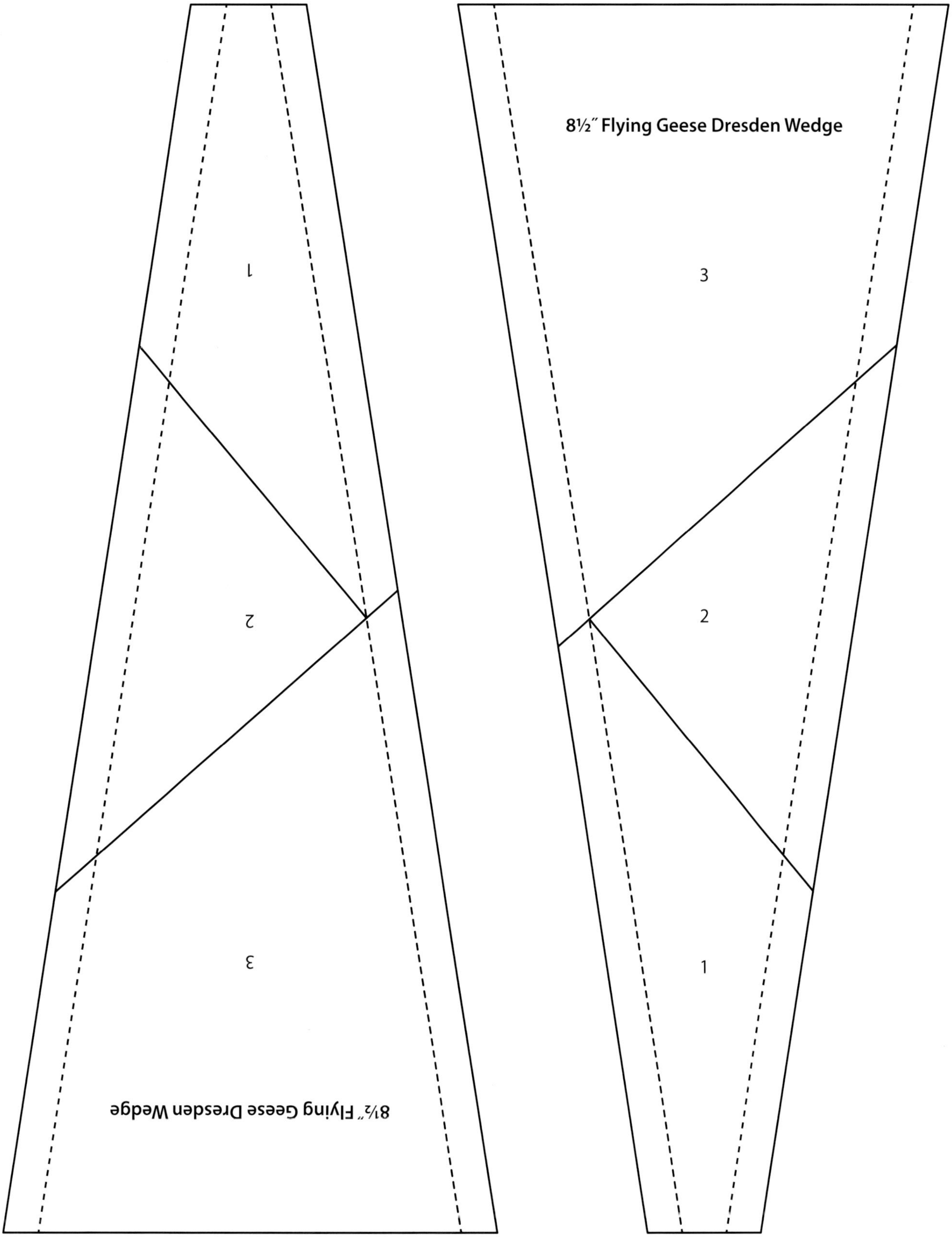
8½″ Flying Geese Dresden Wedge
1
2
3
8½″ Flying Geese Dresden Wedge
3
2
1

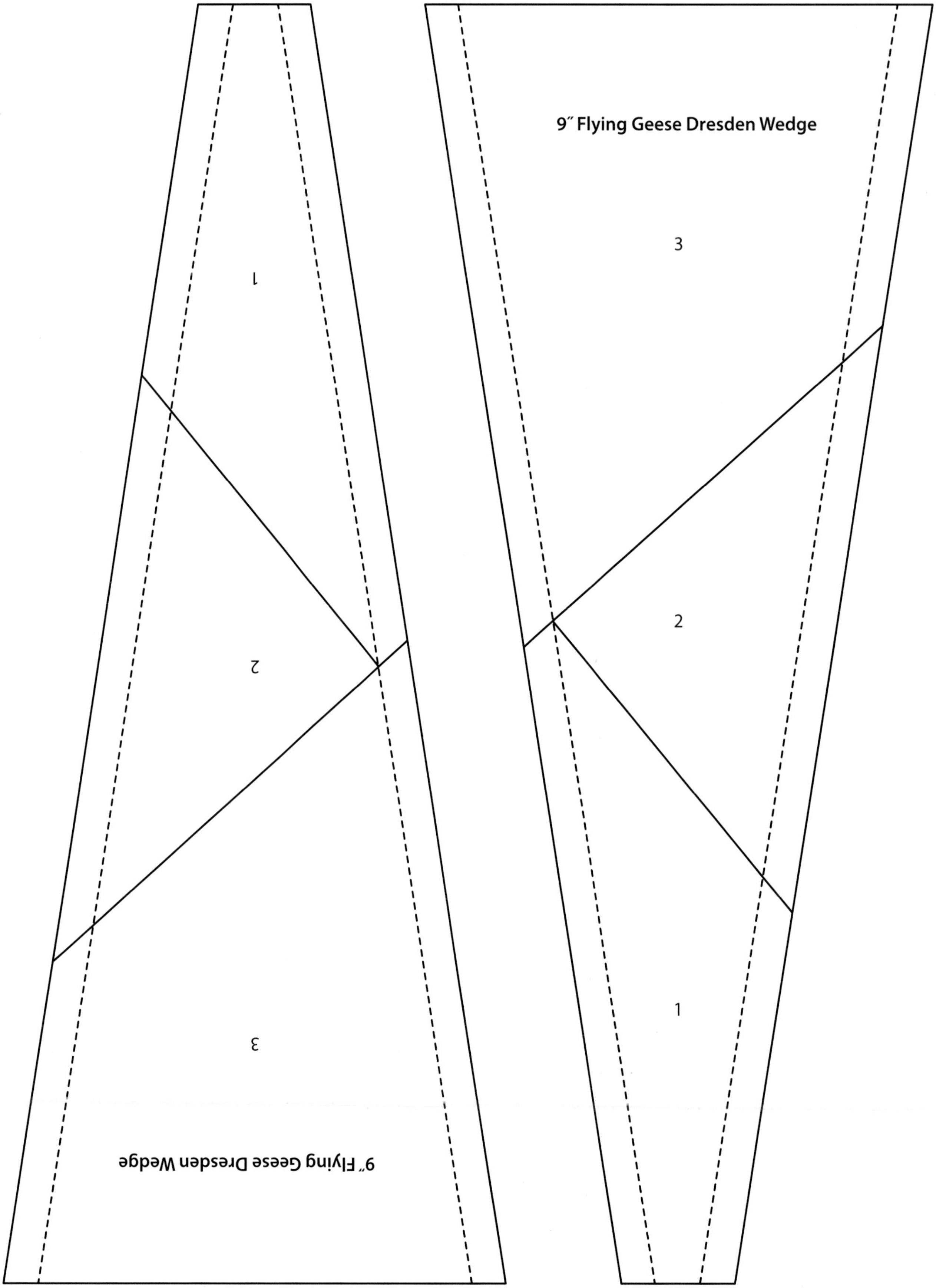
1
2
3
9″ Flying Geese Dresden Wedge
9″ Flying Geese Dresden Wedge
3
2
1

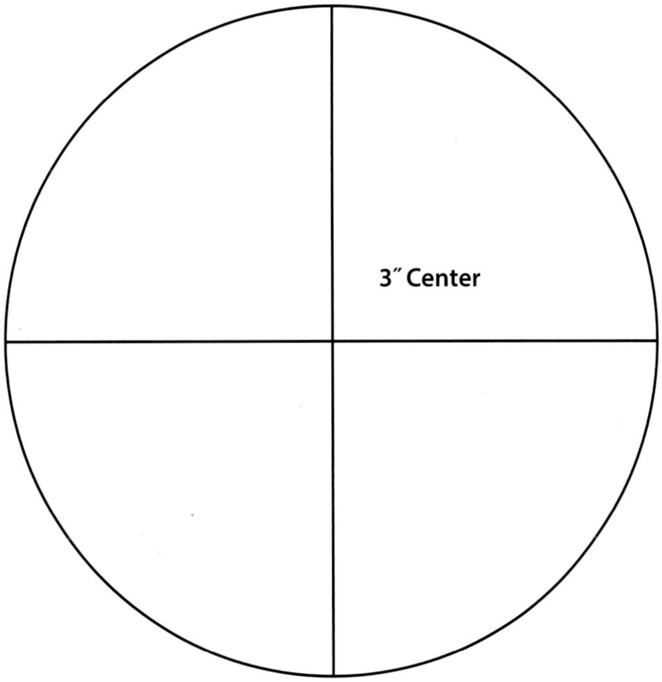
3″ Center

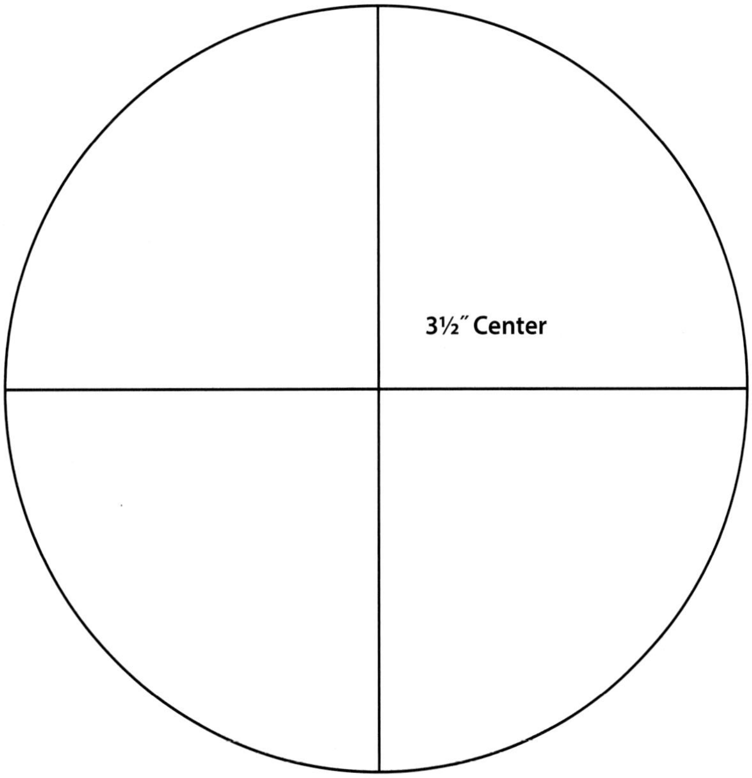
3½″ Center

Resources

Please check with your local quilt shop for these tools and supplies.

Prairie Pointer
piecesbewithyou.com > products
For lining up points on Dresden wedges

Alex Anderson's 4-in-1 Essential Sewing Tool
ctpub.com

Quilter's Freezer Paper Sheets
ctpub.com
For center templates

Carol Doak's Foundation Paper
ctpub.com
For Flying Geese Dresdens

Reynolds Freezer Paper
Available at grocery stores

Goddess Sheet
mistyfuse.com
Nonstick appliqué pressing sheet in various sizes

Pressing Bar
etsy.com > icandyfiberart

Pellon 906F Fusible Sheerweight
pellonprojects.com
Nonwoven lightweight fusible interfacing

Pellon 830 Easy Pattern
pellonprojects.com
Nonwoven interfacing for Dresden centers

Creative Grids 18° Dresden Plate Quilt Ruler
creativegridsusa.com

Wrights Easy Dresden Quilting Ruler

ABOUT THE AUTHOR

I have been fascinated with fabric, sewing and quilting since the age of nine, when I took my first sewing class and won a prize for my corduroy jumper and print shirt with a necktie. When I saw an ancestor's quilt in the Smithsonian at age thirteen, I was hooked. I taught myself to quilt from books and used cardboard templates and scissors to make my first quilt, a Log Cabin. It has been a love affair ever since.

I love using fabrics, themes, and colors from nature, although I lean more and more to bright fabrics with a lot of prints. Many of my works have a "tradition-with-a-twist" quality, and although I rely on inspirations from generations gone by, they also have a contemporary feel. I have dabbled in fiber art, challenges, traditional quilting, and modern quilting, and I love it all.

I have taught quilting for more than twenty years and love the teaching and exploring with students as much as the creating. I have been lucky to have quilts and fiber art pieces juried into shows with Missouri Fiber Artists, the American Quilter's Society in Kentucky, the International Quilt Association in Houston, and the National Quilt Association in Ohio, as well as into many local and regional shows and displays.

I published my first pattern on the Dresden quilt (of course!) in 2015 and look forward to more. I live with my husband, Tom, in both rural Missouri and urban St. Louis with our Golden rescue, Bella. I have two sons who as adults have followed in their father's footsteps, and we couldn't be prouder. They are with wonderful partners, and I hope I will get to pass on some of my love of quilting in their direction.

Photo by Sharon Whitehall of Whitehall Photograph LLC

Candyce Copp Grisham

Visit Candyce online and follow on social media!

Website: icandyfiberart.com

Facebook: /icandyfiberart

Pinterest: /icandyfiberart

Instagram: @icandyfiberart

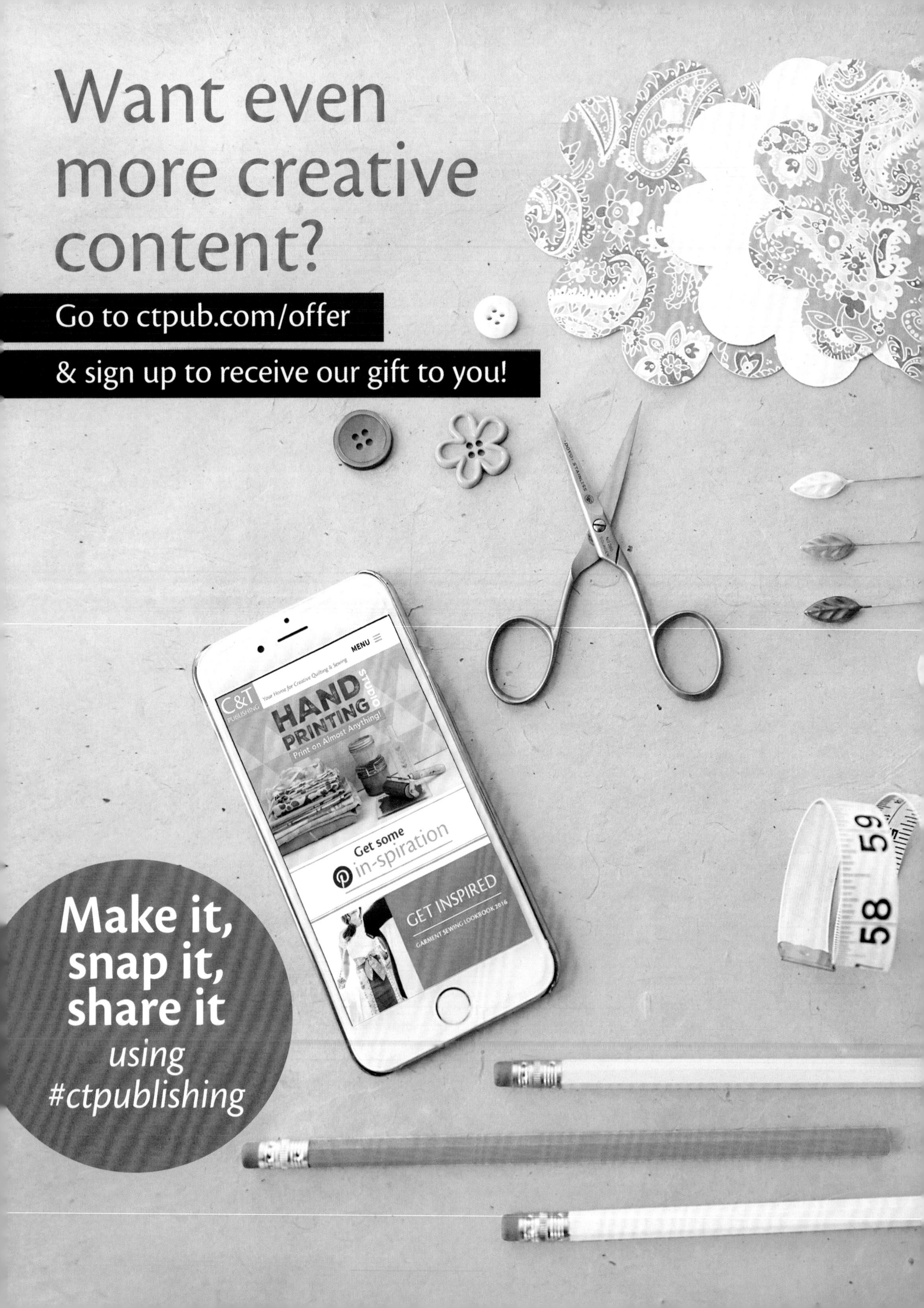
Want even more creative content?
Go to ctpub.com/offer
& sign up to receive our gift to you!
C&T PUBLISHING
Your Home for Creative Quilting & Sewing
MENU
HAND PRINTING STUDIO
Print on Almost Anything!
Get some in-spiration
GET INSPIRED
GARMENT SEWING LOOKBOOK 2016
Make it, snap it, share it
using #ctpublishing